Getting Started in Charitable Gift Planning

The Resource Book

Brian M. Sagrestano, JD, CFRE
Robert E. Wahlers, MS, CFRE

Charity Channel
PRESS

Getting Started in Charitable Gift Planning: The Resource Book

One of the **In the Trenches**™ series

Published by

CharityChannel Press, an imprint of CharityChannel LLC

424 Church Street, Suite 2000

Nashville, TN 37219 USA

CharityChannel.com

ISBN Print Book: 978-1-938077-86-9

Library of Congress Control Number: 2016912970

13 12 11 10 9 8 7 6 5 4 3 2 1

Printed in the United States of America

This and most CharityChannel Press books are available at special quantity discounts for bulk purchases for sales promotions, premiums, fundraising, or educational use. For information, contact CharityChannel Press, 424 Church Street, Suite 2000, Nashville, TN 37219 USA. +1 949-589-5938.

Publisher's Acknowledgments

This book was produced by a team dedicated to excellence; please send your feedback to Editors@ CharityChannel.com.

We first wish to acknowledge the tens of thousands of peers who call CharityChannel.com their online professional home. Your enthusiastic support for the **In the Trenches**™ series is the wind in our sails.

Members of the team who produced this book include:

Editors

Acquisitions: Linda Lysakowski

Editing: Stephen Nill

Production

Layout: Stephen Nill

Design: Deborah Perdue

Administrative

CharityChannel LLC: Stephen C. Nill, CEO

Marketing and Public Relations: John Millen

About the Authors

Brian M. Sagrestano, JD, CFRE

Brian is the president and founder of Gift Planning Development (GPD) LLC, a full-service gift planning consulting firm. He provides gift planning services to a wide range of charitable clients from national organizations focused on high-end philanthropic planning to local charities seeking to start new gift planning programs using his Planned Giving Essentials and Planned Giving In a Box programs. Some of his clients include the University of Notre Dame, Temple University, Create a Jewish Legacy, Harmony Foundation, Bassett Health, The Community Foundation of Herkimer and Oneida Counties, Inc., and Delaware Art Museum. In 2013, Gift Planning Development became a member firm in Constellation Advancement, LLC, a full-service fundraising consulting firm. Prior to starting GPD in 2007, Brian spent twelve years as a charitable gift planner, directing the programs for the University of Pennsylvania, Middlebury College, and Meridian Health Affiliated Foundations.

Brian is a nationally sought-after speaker on gift planning topics, keynoting or presenting at many conferences, including the National Conference on Philanthropic Planning, the National Conference on Planned Giving, the AFP International Conference on Fundraising, the American Council on Gift Annuities Conference, and the Crescendo Practical Planned Giving Conference, as well local and regional conferences around the country. He has taught thousands of fundraisers, professional advisors, board members, and philanthropists how to use a donor-focused approach to integrate philanthropic goals with tax, estate, and financial planning.

A regular contributor to Advancing Philanthropy, Planned Giving Today, Planned Giving Mentor, PlannedGiving.Com, and Planned Giving Tomorrow, Brian has also been cited in numerous publications, including CASE Currents and the Chronicle of Philanthropy. He and Robert coauthored *The Philanthropic Planning Companion—The Fundraisers' and Professional Advisors' Guide to Charitable Gift Planning* (Wiley 2012), the 2013 AFP–Skystone Partners prize winner for research in philanthropy.

Brian is a past board member of the Partnership for Philanthropic Planning (PPP), the Gift Planning Council of New Jersey, and PPP of Greater Philadelphia, as well as a past member of the editorial board of the *Journal of Gift Planning*.

An honors graduate of both Cornell University and Notre Dame Law School, Brian lives with his wife and four children in New Hartford, New York, the scenic gateway to the Adirondack Mountains. In his off hours, Brian sings with the Mohawk Valley Chapter of the Barbershop Harmony Society, an internationally ranked barbershop chorus, as well as his local church choir. He also likes to spend time outdoors, hiking, canoeing, kayaking, and skiing in the Adirondack Park.

To learn more about GPD, Constellation or to share your thoughts with Brian, visit *giftplanningdevelopment.com* or email brian@giftplanningdevelopment.com.

Robert E. Wahlers, MS, CFRE

Robert is the Vice President of Development for Meridian Health Affiliated Foundations, where he oversees the gift planning, annual giving and grants development program for the eight hospitals in the Meridian Health System. During his tenure, he has also served as the Executive Director for Jersey Shore University Medical Center Foundation and K. Hovnanian Children's Hospital. Over his more than twenty-five-year-career, Robert has worked in the financial and estate planning field and in the nonprofit sector with the Boy Scouts of America, the American Cancer Society, Virtua Foundation, and now Meridian Health. Robert learned early on the value of developing relationships with professional advisors and honed those skills while with the American Cancer Society, where he saw how philanthropic planning can be an asset for the donor and the charity.

A speaker to audiences of five to five thousand, Robert has presented at such conferences as the National Conference on Philanthropic Planning, the National Conference on Planned Giving, the Association of Fundraising Professionals International Conference, the Boy Scouts of America All Hands Conference, and the American Cancer Society Distinguished Gifts Conference, as well as several regional and local conferences.

Robert is an honors graduate with a master of science degree in human development and leadership with a concentration in nonprofit management from Murray State University and a bachelor of arts degree in psychology from Muhlenberg College. Robert and Brian coauthored their first book, *The Philanthropic Companion—The Fundraisers' and Professional Advisors' Guide to Charitable Gift Planning,* which was published by Wiley in 2012 and is the 2013 winner of the AFP–Skystone Partners Research Award. He has also been published in *Advancing Philanthropy* and *Planned Giving Today* and has been cited in the *Nonprofit Times,* the *Chronicle of Philanthropy,* and *Advancing Philanthropy,* among others. Robert serves on the faculty at Columbia University in its masters of fundraising management program.

He is a former national board member with the Partnership for Philanthropic Planning (PPP) and is active on several AFP committees. Robert also served on the boards of the Gift Planning Council of New Jersey and the Association of Fundraising Professionals–New Jersey Chapter, where he is a past president. Robert is also active as a 32nd degree York Rite and Scottish Rite Mason and Shriner.

When not working, Robert spends time with his wife and two children at their home at the Jersey Shore or on the Inner Banks of North Carolina. He also enjoys racing wooden sailboats as part of the Barnegat Bay Yacht Racing Association and maintains a studio for illustration and oil painting.

Dedication

To the organizations where we served that inspired us through their missions and gave us the opportunity to work with extraordinary donors who make a lasting difference.

Authors' Acknowledgments

Having already written a comprehensive book on philanthropic planning, our second book and the resource book that supports it are allowing us to get back to the basics that we learned at the early stages of our careers.

All who enter into fundraising need to establish a baseline of knowledge that can serve them throughout their careers. We are both fortunate that our upbringing and values along with our education and early experience prepared us well to absorb the wisdom of those we were fortunate to meet—Diane McConnell, Ben Madonia, Jere Williams, Bill Davis, Bob Sharpe, Jr., Kathryn Miree, Ron Brown, Frank Congilose, Paul Hansen, Charles Schultz, Laura Fredricks, Bill Sturtevant, and Steve Simmonds—each who influenced our development and pointed us on the path toward building our expertise.

We have also been inspired by thousands of donors who were moved by the missions of the organizations we have served and put their faith and trust in us to help them in making gifts to support the Boy Scouts of America, Clarkson University, the American Cancer Society, Middlebury College, Virtua Foundation, Meridian Health Affiliated Foundations and the University of Pennsylvania.

We would like to thank the three gift planners who completed peer reviews of our manuscripts, including Roger Ellison, CFP, Johni Hays, JD, and Kristen Schultz Jaarda, JD. Their thoughtful comments and edits improved the content and flow of these materials. We would also like to thank Stephen Nill, JD, and the team at CharityChannel Press for their help and support throughout the process of putting this book together. Finally, we appreciate the review and thoughtful Foreword by Professor Russell James who continues to lead our field with his outstanding research to support gift planning and fundraising.

We are hopeful that ***Getting Started in Charitable Gift Planning: Your Guide to Planned Giving*** and this associated ***Getting Started in Charitable Gift Planning: Resource Book*** will be a guide to others as they grow in their knowledge to build relationships and assist the donors they serve.

Contents

Summary of Chapters

Gifts That Maximize the Donor's Charitable Legacy Through Beneficiary Designations. Donors have several options to support their favorite charities. Beneficiary designations through wills and living trusts, retirement plans, life insurance policies, and donor-advised funds are a few that are widely used.

Gifts That Provide Income. Charitable gift annuities, pooled income funds, and charitable remainder trusts offer donors the opportunity to give while also receiving an income.

Gifts That Maximize Inheritance. Charitable lead trusts and wealth replacement charitable remainder trusts offer donors an opportunity to make a gift while maximizing what is left for their loved ones.

Gifts of Complex Assets. Art and collectibles, business interests and real estate are a few of the complex assets that may be offered to charities as gifts. Whether it is a life insurance policy or stock, or another appreciated asset, knowing when and how to accept or decline these types of gifts is a necessity in gift planning.

Answers to Common Gift Planning Questions. It is important to understand the basics as you begin your quest for gift planning knowledge. Many of the common questions are answered.

Infrastructure. The internal case, gift counting policy, gift acceptance policy, and gift agreements are presented along with samples and estate administration materials to help manage your gift planning program.

Prospect Interaction. As you become familiar with a new prospect, several attributes are important to understand and explore.

Marketing. Support materials and other resources including a sample marketing grid are presented. Stewardship materials and our seven touches philosophy for stewardship are also covered.

Introduction

Many have enjoyed a hike along the Appalachian Trail. Stretching from Georgia to Maine, the trail is roughly 2,200 miles long. We have known several friends who are thru-hikers meaning they have hiked the entire trail in an extended adventure that takes vision, commitment, planning, skill, strength, endurance, and perseverance. Building a donor-focused gift planning program will require many of the same attributes. While it may not be as physically demanding as hiking the Appalachian Trail, your organization must plan your steps and pursue your program with the same dogged determination.

Like a long hike, you need to understand what you need before you start. Knowing just the basics might get you started, but you could fail quickly and lose interest if you do not plan properly. In the *Getting Started in Charitable Gift Planning Resource Book (Resource Book)*, we will give you the basics, explain the common terms and offer some helpful tools that should allow you to plan for your own program or perhaps just strengthen what you might have inherited when you started in your role. Either way, we hope that this resource will aid you in your journey.

Donor-Focused Charitable Gift Planning

Donor-focused philanthropy is an emerging model for raising funds. Instead of asking what donors can do for nonprofits, it asks what donors need to accomplish for themselves, their families, and their future. It seeks out what is really important to them in their lives, including the legacy they want to build. It then asks how nonprofits they support can be integrated into their tax, estate, and financial planning to help meet these present and future goals. It requires your organization to develop significant relationships with your donors to understand what impact they want to have today, what outcomes they hope to achieve for tomorrow, and what legacy they desire to create during their lifetimes and beyond.

Donor-Focused Gift Charitable Planning

Gift planning is a powerful and meaningful way for individuals to give to charities, ensure their long-term futures, and also meet personal planning objectives. It is the process of cultivating, designing, facilitating, and stewarding gifts. Gift planning uses a variety of financial tools and techniques for giving. It usually requires the assistance of one or more qualified specialists, utilizes tax incentives that encourage charitable giving when appropriate, covers the full spectrum of generosity by individuals and institutions, and is based on powerful traditions of giving in the United States.

—Partnership for Philanthropic Planning

Donor-focused gift planning, or philanthropic planning, provides donors with the ability to meet both their personal planning objectives and their philanthropic goals to craft a more meaningful and lasting legacy. To achieve this goal, you will need to partner with your donors and their advisors, listen to what is important to them, provide the appropriate tools, and support them to help reach this end.

Building the Infrastructure

As fundraisers, we attend classes, seminars, and conferences to gain knowledge in new areas of fundraising, but to implement these strategic ideas and turn them into useful programs can be daunting. While *Getting Started in Charitable Gift Planning* covers the steps needed to move an organization from one that has focused on annual and major giving to one that can include gift planning and have it serve as an integrated component of its development program, this *Resource Book* includes basic tools and templates to assist in the creation of the infrastructure necessary to start a gift planning program.

Interacting with Prospects

Getting Started in Charitable Gift Planning and the *Resource Book* provide fundraisers and nonprofits with the basics of how to identify gift planning prospects and opportunities, have the gift planning conversation, and steward gift planning donors, including our groundbreaking work applying generational cohorts to fundraising strategies. It also defines the different gift planning tools and how to apply them to particular prospect situations. Whether nonprofits are meeting with donors or their professional advisors, fundraisers need the ability to speak the same language and understand the core concepts.

Part One

Deciphering the Alphabet Soup—An Introduction to the Basic Tools of Charitable Gift Planning

As you work with donors and advisors, it is important to understand the concepts and common gift planning tools that are used. Some of the terms and the most common tools are here for you to learn or reference in the future. These tools are a means to an end and should be considered in the context of integrating donors' charitable intentions with their overall tax, estate, and financial plans. As you will come to understand, therein lies the concept of donor-focused charitable gift planning.

The techniques of charitable gift planning include revocable and irrevocable arrangements, gifts available for use at the time they are given, gifts that may not be available until a future date, and split-interest gifts intended to balance financial, personal, and charitable objectives.

Donors should seek charitable gift planning advice from professionals with integrity, expertise, and experience in law, investments, property, tax, and charitable transfers to ensure the technical aspects of the transfer and the philanthropic quality of the gift. Similarly, fundraisers should strive to work with professional advisors to assist them in their work with donors.

Generally, gift planning programs are built in stages as outlined in the four chapters in this section.

Gift Planning Program Stages

Stage I: Bequests & Testamentary Gifts (Revocable)

Stage I programs are the starting point for most gift planning programs. Donors articulate their philanthropic intentions through the use of a will, trust, or other written instrument (often as simple as filling out a form). Bequests and testamentary gifts include gifts from:

- ◆ Wills (Bequests)
- ◆ Revocable Living Trusts
- ◆ Retirement Plans

- Life Insurance Policies

- Donor-Advised Funds (DAF)

- Payable-on-Death Accounts (POD)

- Transfer-on-Death Accounts and Assets (TOD)

The gift to charity is revocable and will not occur until after the death of the donor. In addition to the satisfaction derived from making an important gift to charity, there may be significant tax/financial benefits for donors' estates. We discuss the components of the Stage I program in Chapter One.

Stage II: Gifts that Provide Income and Meet Personal Planning Objectives (Irrevocable)

Stage II gift planning programs feature charitable arrangements that provide income to help donors meet personal planning objectives, such as increasing income in retirement or providing for an elderly parent or loved one. The vehicles used typically produce payments for them (or someone they name) for life or a term of years. After the payment beneficiary has died, or at the end of a term of years, the gift ends and the fund balance is distributed to charities named in the arrangement.

Examples include:

- Charitable Gift Annuity (CGA)

- Pooled Income Fund (PIF)

- Charitable Remainder Trust (CRT)

Life-income gifts have potential benefits for the donor, including:

- Avoidance of capital gains taxes

- Increased income

- Income tax deduction

- Probate/estate expense reduction

- Professional financial management, and

- The satisfaction derived from making a significant gift to charity

We discuss the Stage II charitable arrangements in Chapter Two.

Stage III: Gifts to Maximize Inheritance

Stage III gift planning programs truly integrate donors' philanthropic goals with their tax, estate, and financial planning using a philanthropic planning methodology that we discuss in our book: *The Philanthropic Planning Companion: The Fundraisers' and Professional Advisors' Guide to Charitable Gift Planning* (Wiley 2012). Such programs use the full range of tools available to meet donor needs, including:

- Wealth replacement trust

- Charitable lead trust

We cover these charitable tools in **Chapter Three.**

These conversations also include gifts of complex assets, since most high-net-worth philanthropists hold a wide range of assets and are often entrepreneurs. We discuss different types of complex assets and how to use them for charitable giving in **Chapter Four.**

Chapter One

Gifts That Maximize the Donor's Charitable Legacy Through Beneficiary Designations

IN THIS CHAPTER

- ···→ Encourage gifts from wills (bequests) and revocable living trusts

- ···→ Suggest gifts from qualified retirement plans and life insurance policies

- ···→ Consider gifts from donor-advised funds

- ···→ Remember gifts from payable-on-death accounts and transfer-on-death assets

The simplest, most common planned or legacy gifts are created through beneficiary designations on wills, trusts, retirement plans, life insurance policies, donor-advised funds, payable-on-death accounts, and transfer-on-death accounts/assets. Together they make up over 80 percent of all gift planning revenue raised by charities each year.

While most gift planning books, seminars, and educational materials focus on complicated gift plans, the reality is that if you spend your time building or growing a Stage I gift planning program, which just covers beneficiary designations, you will do more for your organization than a highly technical gift planner using the more complex tools described in **Chapters Two, Three,** and **Four**. More importantly, you will help far more donors realize their philanthropic goals while also supporting your cause. Best of all, beneficiary designations are easy to understand and explain so you can readily share this information with all of the donors loyal to your organization.

Beneficiary designations can be outright, for specific assets, residual, and contingent. Each option allows your donor to provide for loved ones while also supporting your charity. Donors should select the type of beneficiary designation that makes the most sense for their situation. As the representative of the charity, your role is to make them aware of the different options and suggest that they consult with their own advisors when determining what is best in their situation.

Bequests

Bequests account for about 8 percent of the total charitable contributions from Americans annually.

—Giving USA

observation

Wills

Naming your organization as the beneficiary of a will is the most basic form of planned gift and the foundation for your gift planning program. A gift through a will (bequest intention) allows the donor to transfer personal property, such as stocks, bonds, jewelry, or cash, to your organization. When real estate is left through a will, it is correctly called a "devise."

When your organization is named as a beneficiary of a will, it is often called a legacy gift. Donors have several options in addition to giving directly through a will. Donors may also give to a charity by using a revocable living trust (living trust) that would first accomplish personal planning goals for the donor before benefiting your organization. Both are legal documents that specify how property will be distributed at death, but a living trust also helps the donor to manage property during life. A donor can benefit your organization by including a provision in the original will when it is drafted or can amend an existing plan by executing an amendment called a "codicil" (for a will) or a "trust amendment" (for a living trust).

A donor can give a specific dollar amount or asset (a specific bequest) or a percentage of their residuary estate (a residuary bequest). It can be paid outright, or it can be made dependent on whether the primary beneficiary (like a spouse or child) is living at the time the bequest is realized. The donor can specify how the bequest is to be used—for unrestricted or specific purposes, outright, or endowed. Any amounts passing to charity will pass free of estate tax in the donor's estate.

Sample Will Beneficiary Language

Prospects and their advisors will frequently visit your website in search of your legal name, address, tax identification number, and sample language to name your organization as a beneficiary of a will, living trust, or other legacy gift. For wills, the following language is fairly typical:

Specific Gift Language

I give and devise to [YOUR NONPROFIT], tax identification number [TAX ID NUMBER] located in [CITY AND STATE], or its successor, the sum of $[AMOUNT OF GIFT] (or [DESCRIPTION OF ASSET]) to be used where it determines the need is greatest (or for the support of a specific fund or program).

Residual Bequest Language

I give and devise to [YOUR NONPROFIT], tax identification number [TAX ID NUMBER], located in [CITY AND STATE], all (or state a percentage) of the rest, residue, and remainder of my estate, both real and personal, to be used where it determines the need is greatest (or for the support of a specific fund or program).

Note: This publication cannot provide tax or legal advice. Your organization should consult with legal counsel before providing sample bequest language to your donors, particularly to ensure compliance with state and federal laws. All sample materials throughout the *Resource Book* are provided as a starting point for those conversations.

Example

Because your charity has a particular mission and must apply donated funds according to certain guidelines and rules, and because the donor's bequest might not be received until after many years have passed, it is important to encourage the donor to confer with your organization about a proposed restricted purpose prior to including it in the will, to ensure that your organization can administer the bequest according to the donor's wishes both now and in the future, particularly for endowed gifts.

Please note that restricted bequests appeal to donors, but bequests designated for your general purposes give your organization the most flexibility to meet its needs when the bequest is realized. The best solution is flexible language that allows your organization to repurpose restricted bequests if your organization can no longer use the gift as the donor intended.

Living Trusts

A "revocable inter vivos trust," also known as a living trust, is created by a living individual (grantor) to manage assets for the benefit of the grantor and, possibly, other persons during the grantor's lifetime. The grantor has the right to modify or revoke the trust during life.

At the grantor's death, the living trust becomes irrevocable and its assets are distributed to named beneficiaries, either outright or in further trust just as they would be under a will. However, assets held in the trust are "nonprobate" assets, and trust distributions are not overseen by a probate court. Typically, the grantor serves as the initial trustee of the living trust and appoints an additional trustee to oversee the distributions of assets after passing.

As noted earlier, naming your organization as the beneficiary of a living trust produces the same result as naming your organization as the beneficiary of a will. The mechanics are slightly different, but competent legal counsel can assist your donor in modifying the sample will beneficiary language to include in a new living trust or a trust amendment.

> ### Benjamin Franklin's Testamentary Trusts
>
> Well-known patriot Benjamin Franklin set up two trusts in his Last Will that was written in 1788 and became effective in 1789 that allocated £1,000 for the purpose of providing low-interest loans to "artificers" (former apprentices in various trades) with funds to enable them to go into their own businesses. He directed that, after one hundred years, about 70 percent of the trust was to be distributed to support public works, such as bridges, aqueducts, fortifications, and public buildings. After two hundred years, estimating that the trust would then be worth about £4 million, he directed that it distribute the balance to communities. In 1991, the trust in Philadelphia distributed over $2.2 million to the community foundation and the Franklin Institute, just as Franklin had directed in his will.
>
>

Qualified Retirement Plans and IRAs

Qualified retirement plans such an IRA, 401k, 403b, and pension offer an easy option for donors to consider when making a charitable gift at death. Given that the funds in qualified retirement plans have never been taxed, these plans are typically the best assets to designate for estate gifts to charity, with other assets benefiting heirs and friends.

Retirement assets will be considered "income in respect of a decedent" in a donor's estate, which means that they will be subject to income tax in their estate or the hands of their beneficiaries, including a spouse. Also, if the assets are left to beneficiaries other than a spouse, they will be subject to estate tax. This double taxation can consume up to 70 percent of the value of a distribution from a retirement plan to the children of the deceased plan participant (your donor). However, a distribution to your organization or another charity passes free of both income and estate tax.

Your donor can actually preserve more of the value of their estate for heirs by using retirement assets for their charitable gifts and other assets for their heirs.

To name your organization as the beneficiary of a retirement plan, your donor should request a change of beneficiary form from the retirement plan provider. In most cases, the form will require the legal name, address, and tax identification number of your organization.

Most plan providers will allow your donor to name your organization for only a percentage of the plan assets. Because this can sometimes become complicated, we typically recommend that the donor split the plan into two, naming your organization the total beneficiary of its first part, and different beneficiaries of the other part. It helps avoid any issues with distributions to heirs upon the death of the donor.

If your donor wants to restrict the use of the proceeds from the retirement plan, we also suggest that you execute a nonbinding statement of intent with your donor describing the use of the funds from the retirement plan. Documenting your donor's wishes is the best way to ensure that they are carried out. If a formal statement of intent is not possible, a letter of direction signed by your donor is helpful in guiding future use of the funds. Ideally, any such direction will also include saving language allowing you to use the funds for another purpose if the designation is no longer practicable in the future.

Life Insurance

Life insurance can serve as a wonderful tool to meet many financial planning and charitable giving needs (described in more detail in Chapter Four). But for a donor who no longer needs an existing life insurance policy, naming your organization as the beneficiary can be an excellent use of this resource.

To name your organization as a beneficiary of a life insurance policy, much like with a retirement plan, your donor should request a change of beneficiary form from the policy provider. The donor then designates your organization to receive the proceeds using your legal name, address, and tax identification number.

Donor-Advised Funds

A Donor-Advised Fund (DAF) is charitable giving account offered through an organization recognized as a public charity under federal tax law. You may be familiar with the Fidelity Charitable Gift Fund, the Schwab Charitable Fund, Vanguard Charitable, the National Philanthropic Trust, the Dechomai Foundation, or a DAF held at your local community foundation, often referred to as "umbrella" DAFs.

To create an individual DAF, a donor establishes a separate fund at the "umbrella" DAF by making an irrevocable contribution of cash, securities, or other assets to the umbrella DAF's trustee. The trustee will review the recommended grants and make a determination of whether to follow the donor's recommendations. The donor cannot direct the trustee to make a particular grant, and the trustee has the right to override donor advice regarding the timing or recipient of a gift. Your donor's DAF administrator will provide appropriate paperwork on which to submit distribution advice. If the organization is based in the United States and qualifies as a charitable organization, the trustee typically will not override the donor's advice.

DAF grants may not be used to satisfy preexisting, binding, charitable pledges. It may be possible to use a DAF to satisfy nonbinding statements of intent. Because the assets held in your donor's DAF are the property of the DAF, your client will not receive an additional income tax charitable deduction for any amount the DAF trustee agrees to distribute to charity.

At the end of 2013, when Congress held hearings about potentially scaling back the income tax charitable deduction, many individuals created or made significant additions to their existing DAFs, to claim full deductions before any changes to the tax code that would limit deductions. Even though that provision never passed, there are now more funds in DAFs than ever before, which can benefit your organization through current and legacy gifts. For legacy gifts, this is an underutilized resource.

When the DAF fund creator dies, most DAFs allow for

◆ a successor fund holder to be named to continue to recommend distributions (but often this is only allowed for one generation);

◆ an ultimate charitable beneficiary to be named to receive the remaining funds; or

◆ the umbrella fund to designate use of the remainder for charitable purposes without further input from the fund creator.

However, rarely are these options advertised or discussed with fund creators.

With the significant assets now held in DAFs, it is wise to recommend to your donors that they consider naming your organization as the beneficiary of the remaining funds in the DAF. It is a simple form that can be requested from the DAF administrator that names your organization as the requested, ultimate beneficiary of the DAF.

Payable-on-Death Accounts

A payable-on-death account (POD) is a bank account that allows individuals to pass the funds remaining in the account at death directly to account beneficiaries outside of the probate process. This means that these assets are not controlled by a will or revocable living trust, but by the contractual arrangement between the account owner and financial institution. PODs are regulated by state law, but generally bank accounts, CDs, and savings bonds qualify for POD treatment in most jurisdictions.

The dramatic increase in POD beneficiary designations was noted by Russell James (*http://encouragegenerosity.com/research_papers.htm*) in his recent research on legacy giving. He suggests that, over time, beneficiary designations on retirement plans, living trusts, life insurance, PODs and transfer-on-death assets (contractual alternatives) will become much more important to charities than gifts from wills. We have noted this trend for several years, as well. As fewer assets are left to go through the probate process (pass under

---

DAF Alternatives

DAFs are part of a larger group of charitable giving tools which are designed to assist individuals who want to formalize and structure their charitable giving. These tools include DAFs, supporting organizations, and private foundations. Ultimately your organization can also be named as the final beneficiary of each of these legal entities if that is how the donor sets up the governing documents. If your donor has a private foundation or a supporting organization, an amendment to the governing document may be required to name your organization as the ultimate beneficiary. But as the dollars in these alternative organizations can be substantial, when a donor mentions a supporting organization or private foundation, it is important to discuss if there is interest in naming your organization as a beneficiary.

observation

the will) because of contractual alternatives, charities will need to change their focus to these alternatives if they want to keep their legacy giving programs robust.

As with the other contractual alternatives, naming your organization as a beneficiary of a POD requires a simple form from the account administrator in which the account owner names your organization as the beneficiary. Upon the donor's death, you make a claim by presenting an original death certificate or asking the estate administrator to do so.

Transfer-on-Death Accounts and Assets

Similar to a POD, a transfer-on-death account (TOD) is an investment account that allows individuals to pass the assets remaining in the account at death directly to named beneficiaries, including charities, outside of the probate process using a beneficiary designation form.

Relatively recently, some states have begun to allow transfer-on-death designations in real estate deeds, whereby the property passes outside of the probate process to the ultimate beneficiary. While still not available in all states, it does allow a donor to pass real estate directly to your organization upon death without probate and without a retained life estate. Such a provision requires the designation to be recorded on the deed and may require additional filings with the state to actually make the transfer. But if your donors are like many individuals, the largest asset owned may be real estate so a transfer to your organization at death might be the largest gift the donor can make and is worth exploring.

To Recap

◆ Beneficiary designations on wills, trusts, retirement plans, and life insurance policies can provide the donor with a simple way to support your organization.

◆ Naming your organization as the ultimate beneficiary of a donor-advised fund is an emerging way to allow your donor to direct dollars that have already been earmarked for charity to your organization, rather than allowing the fund sponsor to decide which organizations should benefit.

◆ Payable-on-death accounts and transfer-on-death accounts/assets have long been overlooked as easy assets to pass to your organization without needing to involve an attorney. With an increased number of states allowing for real estate to pass using a transfer-on-death deed, it is another emerging tool you can recommend to your donors.

◆ If you focused your effort only on encouraging gifts from these common tools that offer beneficiary designations in a Stage I gift planning program, you will help a far greater number of donors to realize their philanthropic goals while also supporting your cause.

Chapter Two

Gifts that Provide Income

IN THIS CHAPTER

- ⋯➔ Understanding charitable gift annuities and how they work

- ⋯➔ Be aware of pooled income funds

- ⋯➔ Consider opportunities for developing gifts from charitable remainder trusts

- ⋯➔ Donor-focused planning may lead to more sophisticated trust options

Prospects will often declare, "I would like to help your cause, but..." where "but" is some financial planning need that must be resolved for the prospect to move forward with the gift. These can include things like needing more income during retirement, providing income to an elderly parent or loved one, or helping to pay for a college education for grandchildren.

A Stage II donor-focused gift planning program provides an opportunity to help these individuals overcome their financial challenges by providing charitable giving solutions that both meet the financial planning need while at the same time also providing a charitable gift to support your organization.

In this chapter, we describe variations on three charitable giving tools: the charitable gift annuity, the pooled income fund, and the charitable remainder trust. Each of these tools has unique characteristics that make them appropriate for different donor planning needs. By selecting the best tool, donors can make a gift to advance their charitable objectives while also meeting the needs of family members in as tax-efficient a way as possible. It is the "win-win" of charitable gift planning and something for which to strive when working with your donors. Not only will they appreciate your interest in helping them meet their goals, it often has the added benefit of leaving additional assets for future gifts.

Charitable Gift Annuities

Charitable gift annuities are one of the most commonly offered charitable giving tools to meet personal planning objectives. They are a simple contract between the donor and a charity. In exchange for the irrevocable gift of cash, securities, or other assets, the charity agrees to pay one or two annuitants (if a second is named) a fixed sum each year for life. The payments are secured by the general resources of the charity.

The older the annuitants are at the time of the gift, the greater the fixed payments will be that is paid to the donor by the charity. In most cases, part of each payment is tax free, which increases each payment's after-tax value. Payments are usually made annually, semiannually, quarterly, or monthly based on the donor's preference.

Charitable gift annuities are tremendously flexible. They can allow for immediate or deferred payments, commuted payments for a particular purpose, or payments that start when the payment beneficiary needs the distributions. They can be established during life or through a will (testamentary gift annuity). In all cases, the donor benefits from an immediate income tax charitable deduction for a portion of the funding amount, . When the donor uses appreciated stock to fund a gift annuity, a portion of the capital gain attributable to the stock is also avoided.

Why Offer Charitable Gift Annuities?

Charitable gift annuities (CGAs or gift annuities) allow donors to provide greater support for a charity's mission because the donor can retain or assign the right to payments while using the asset to make a charitable gift. For most gift annuity donors, if the gift annuity option is not available, the gift to charity would be deferred until later or even until death because the donor needs a portion of the assets being used to meet a personal planning goal. These mission-based gifts allow donors to make larger gifts today than they otherwise could while also meeting personal planning objectives.

The most common use for a gift annuity is to assist the donor in increasing income in retirement while also supporting a cause important to the donor. For example, a donor can use a low dividend (2 percent) stock to fund a gift annuity and increase the payments to a much higher amount while making a charitable gift. When the tax benefits of an income tax charitable deduction and capital gains tax deferral are included in the calculation, the benefit to the donor is even greater. Other uses of charitable gift annuities include providing support to an elderly parent or loved one, helping with tuition, and, for younger donors, to supplement retirement savings in a tax-deferred way. For some donors from the Depression and World War II generations, simply knowing that they have the income from a gift annuity, even if it is not needed, allows them to make a charitable gift now rather than waiting until their death.

Types of Charitable Gift Annuities and How They Work

A charitable gift annuity is a contractual arrangement between a donor and a charity, regulated by the donor's state of residence and the home state of the organization. In exchange for the donor's gift (normally in the form of cash, appreciated stock or other readily marketable assets), the charity agrees to provide one or two payment beneficiaries with annuity payments for life. (Typically, at least one payment beneficiary is the donor, but this is not required.) Upon the death of the last payment beneficiary, any assets remaining (the residuum) are available for use by the charity for the purpose designated by the donor (or for its unrestricted use if the donor has not designated the use of the residuum).

The donor benefits from an income tax charitable deduction equal to the present value of the future gift to the charity. In real terms, this means that the income tax deduction is the value of amount used to fund the gift annuity, reduced by the present value of the right to payments that the annuity will make.

Payments from a charitable gift annuity are usually taxable to the person receiving them. When funded with cash, a portion of each payment is taxable at ordinary income tax rates with the balance of the payment treated as a tax-free return of principal. When the charitable gift annuity is funded with appreciated assets, such as stock, a portion of each payment is generally taxed at ordinary income tax rates with a portion at capital gains tax rates. In some cases, a portion may also be a tax-free return of principal. If the donor uses appreciated assets to fund a gift annuity but is not one of the annuitants, the donor will owe some capital gains tax upon the funding of the gift annuity.

There are four types of charitable gift annuities: immediate payment, deferred payment, flexible payment, and commuted payment. Each provides unique opportunities for the donor to meet personal planning needs while also supporting your charitable mission.

Immediate Payment Gift Annuities

By far the most common type of gift annuity, the immediate payment CGA provides for immediate payments once the donor transfers assets to charity and executes a contract. Donors seeking to increase their current retirement income from low-yielding assets are the most likely to seek out an immediate payment gift annuity. In some cases, when an elderly parent or loved one needs supplemental support, a family member may set up an immediate payment CGA to provide payments to the parent. This helps avoid the difficult dynamic of an older family member accepting a check from a younger family member, as the funds are direct-deposited in the account of the older family member by the charity. Whenever a gift annuity benefits someone other than the donor, gift tax must be taken into consideration.

Deferred Payment Gift Annuities

The deferred payment CGA provides for distributions starting at least one year in the future. The start date for payments is set by the donor when the annuity contract is signed. The more distant the start of payments is set in the future, the greater the annuity payout rate. Because the principal used to fund the annuity has time to grow without any withdrawals, deferred payment CGAs typically result in a larger residuum for charity than an immediate payment CGA. Deferred payment CGAs are most often used to supplement retirement savings for younger donors and to help defray future anticipated expenses. For some donors, it is just the security of knowing that money is available to them in the future, even if they may not need it.

Flexible Payment Gift Annuities

The flexible payment CGA is similar to the deferred payment CGA. It provides for distributions starting at least one year in the future. However, unlike the deferred payment CGA, with a flexible payment CGA the donor and the charity agree upon a period of years during which the payments might start. For example, if the donor plans to retire in the next five to ten years, the flexible payment DCGA might be set up so payments can start at any time during that five- to ten-year window. The longer into the five- to ten-year window the donor waits to start payments, the higher the payout rate. However, the income tax charitable deduction is calculated based upon the first year the donor would be eligible to receive payments (year five in this example), even if payments are not actually started until later in the period.

Commuted Payment Gift Annuities

The commuted payment CGA is another type of deferred payment CGA. Instead of making payments over the lifetimes of the named payment beneficiaries, the commuted payment CGA takes all of those payments (based on the life expectancies of the payment beneficiaries) and "scrunches" them up into a shorter timeframe, starting at least one year after the annuity is established. The most common use for a commuted payment gift annuity is to meet a future income need that will be short-lived. For example, a donor may set up a commuted payment gift annuity to provide payments for the years that a child is in college, commonly referred to as a "Tuition Annuity" in charitable circles. Another common use is to provide income to the early retiree at age sixty until Social Security kicks in, perhaps age sixty-seven. At the end of the commuted payment period, the annuity terminates and the residuum is available to the charity. The commuted payment CGA is not a term of years gift annuity (which is not permitted in any state). Rather it is a deferred CGA in which the payments which would normally be made over a lifetime are all made in a short window to meet a personal planning need of the donor. Note that commuted payment CGAs are not permitted in New York.

Setting Payout Rates for Charitable Gift Annuities

Absent government regulation, the payout rate on a charitable gift annuity is a negotiation between the charity and the donor. However, as the Federal government and states have moved to regulate gift annuities, they have started to cap rates to protect the charities from offering high payout gift annuities which the charity may not be able to afford.

Since 1927, the American Council on Gift Annuities (ACGA) has provided charities with recommended rates when offering gift annuities. These rates typically meet all of the requirements of federal and state regulations. However, a charity should always check (using readily available software and on-line calculators) to ensure that the rate offered complies with current regulations. Many regulating states will require a charity to get an actuary to determine if a rate is acceptable should the charity offer rates higher than those suggested by the ACGA. Lower rates do not require an actuary. Because of the complexity in determining if higher rates overcome regulatory burdens, the ACGA rates have become the industry standard for maximum rates.

The ACGA rates are determined by an actuary using the following assumptions:

◆ *Target Residuum*—The ACGA rates assume a target residuum of 50 percent, meaning that if the payment beneficiaries live to life expectancy and the other assumptions work out, 50 percent of the original contribution will be available for the charity. The ACGA rates further require that the present value of the residuum be at least 20 percent of the original contribution amount, using the federal government's income tax charitable deduction calculation methodology to determine present value. This effectively reduces the recommended rates for younger payment beneficiaries and should make it so most recommended rates comply with the federal government's 10 percent minimum present value of the residuum. In real terms, this means that if a donor funds a $10,000 gift annuity, the rate should be such that the remainder when the annuity ends should be $5,000 for the charity and the income tax charitable deduction for the donor should not be less than $2,000.

◆ *Mortality*—All payment beneficiaries are assumed to be female and one year younger than their actual ages, based on 2000 Mortality Tables. The ACGA also incorporates a table for increasing life expectancies using a scale provided by the actuary. This assumption helps to account for the fact that most gift annuitants are well-educated and get quality health care, which tends to extend their life expectancies beyond the norm. In gift planning circles, a common quip is that the best way to add years to your life is to take out a charitable gift annuity with your favorite charity.

◆ *Expenses*—Assumed annual expenses for investment and administration of gift annuity assets are 1.0 percent. Beyond the actual investment costs, gift annuities have administrative costs as charities must comply with federal and state regulations, distribute payments, and issue Form 1099 to each payment beneficiary every year.

◆ *Investment Return*—The ACGA rates model a portfolio with growth and fixed income investments resulting in an assumed total return of 4.25 percent per annum (net 3.25 percent after expenses). Some states heavily regulate how gift annuity assets may be invested, which provides security but can also be a drag on performance. Charities issuing gift annuities in multiple states often have several gift annuity investment pools so that they can meet these requirements.

◆ *Payments*—The ACGA rates assume that all payments are made quarterly at the end of the payment period.

Additional factors are used to calculate deferred, flexible, and commuted payment rates. For more information on the ACGA rates, please visit *acga-web.org*.

State Regulation of Charitable Gift Annuities

States have become increasingly vigilant in regulating charitable gift annuities. States generally take four approaches to gift annuities. Nearly a third of all states require registration to issue gift annuities, plus annual filings. As noted, several states also regulate how gift annuity reserve accounts can be invested and they require specific language in gift annuity agreements. Eleven states require charities to register to issue gift annuities, but do not require ongoing reports each year. Eighteen states have criteria that charities must meet to issue gift annuities to residents of their state, but there is no filing requirement. Five states are silent regarding gift annuity regulation.

Most regulating states require charities soliciting gift annuities in their state to comply with their regulations. In practice, most charities do not comply with these regulations when they are soliciting, but wait until they are ready to issue a gift annuity to a person in a regulated state. There are several firms that can assist charities in registering and remaining in compliance with state regulations. Even with the help of such firms, substantial time and effort will likely be required by staff and volunteers to stay in compliance if an organization wishes to issue CGAs in more than one state, due to the diversity of requirements and information needed from the charity.

Some charities do not comply with state gift annuity regulations; instead, they comply only with the regulations in their home state. They argue that because the gift annuity is issued in the home state, the residence of the donor does not matter. Many regulating states will fine charities $10,000 or more per gift annuity contract, plus issue a cease-and-desist letter if they discover a noncompliant charity issuing gift annuities to their residents. If a charity solicits or issues gift annuities outside of its home state and elects not to comply with other state regulations, it should obtain a written legal opinion as to why such compliance is not required. For the most up to date information on state regulations, visit the American Council on Gift Annuities website at *acga-web.org*.

Risks Associated with Charitable Gift Annuities

When a charity issues gift annuities, there are several risks that the charity must manage, including:

Donors Appreciate Immediate Payment Gift Annuities

Over my career, I have been amazed by how many donors come to appreciate immediate payment gift annuities. When I asked why they liked them, they said they are comfortable with the process and like receiving the regular checks from the charity that they hold dear. One donor was able to pay utility bills with the regular income.

—Robert

stories from the real world

◆ *Investment Risk*—Returns from the gift annuity investment pool may average less than the 4.25 percent in the ACGA assumptions. All investments have inherent risk. This can significantly impact the performance of the gift annuity pool, even causing depletion of the reserve associated with the particular annuity. The charity would still be required to make remaining annuity payments from general funds in such cases.

◆ *Longevity Risk*—The payment beneficiaries live longer than the life expectancy in the ACGA assumptions. Even though charities refer to their gift annuity investments as a pool, they typically do not use them as such. Most charities immediately remove the residuum for a particular gift annuity from the gift annuity pool when the gift annuity ends or "matures." This means that when gift annuities terminate sooner than expected, those "windfalls" are not in the pool to help offset those annuities that continue beyond the expected term. This can be an especially significant risk if the gift annuity pool has just a few payment beneficiaries, or one payment beneficiary makes up most of the pool. For example, if a charity has a $2 million pool, but $1.5 million is all on one payment beneficiary and that person lives to age one hundred, the gift annuity program is at substantial risk.

◆ *Timing Risk*—Poor investment returns occur in the early years of a particular gift annuity. Because a gift annuity is funded all at one time, if a donor makes a gift just before a big market decline, it is unlikely that the gift annuity will ever recover. For example, a donor funds a $100,000 gift annuity paying 5 percent ($5,000 per year), and then the value of the investments drops by 50 percent to $50,000. To continue to make the payments, the gift annuity must now pay an effective rate of 10 percent of its assets (10 percent of $50,000 = $5,000 payment). With state investment regulations, it is unlikely that the gift annuity will ever catch up, and, in fact, will rather rapidly deplete, leaving the charity to make payments from other assets.

These risks can result in charities realizing far less than the 50 percent residuum predicted by the ACGA. On the other hand, if investments outperform (particularly in the early years of an annuity), payment beneficiaries do not outlive life expectancy, and/or market timing works in the charity's favor, the charity may see a significant windfall above the 50 percent predicted residuum from maturing gift annuity arrangements. In the 1990s, it was not uncommon for gift annuities to mature with 100-150 percent of the original funding amount as a residuum, but more recently residuums have declined overall.

Responsibilities When Issuing Charitable Gift Annuities

The charity issuing charitable gift annuities has several important responsibilities for asset management and administration that require internal staff expertise or outside professional help.

◆ *Contracts*—Each gift annuity requires the charity to execute a contract with the donor. The contract must comply with the laws of the state of the donor's residence. There are software programs (Crescendo Interactive, PG Calc, and PhilanthroTec are the most common) that can be purchased to provide the proper language for each state. In addition, the contract must properly account for the parties involved and ownership of the assets. For example, if a husband and wife set up a gift annuity for both of their lives, using an asset only owned by the wife, the charity needs to discuss with the donors and their advisors whether to transfer the assets into joint name and use a joint and survivor contract, or if a successor beneficiary contract would be preferable from a tax and estate planning perspective. The charity needs to be aware of the options or it could result in unexpected tax liability for the couple down the road, especially if the parties should later divorce. The contract also includes information about the final use of the gift after the gift annuity matures.

◆ *Calculations*—Before setting up a gift annuity, most donors will request a sample calculation, illustrating the annuity payout rate, income tax charitable deduction, the taxation of gift annuity payments and expected residuum for the charity. Once the gift annuity is completed, donors will expect a final calculation of the gift that they can use in the preparation of their tax documents. The same software programs used for the contracts also provide these calculations.

◆ *1099-Rs*—By January 31 of each year, the issuing charity needs to provide all payment beneficiaries with form 1099-R, indicating how much was distributed and the taxation of payments. There is a separate software package that can be purchased to provide these tax documents.

◆ *Payout Rates*—As noted, each charity determines its own maximum payout rates (typically capped by the ACGA rates), but can also offer lower rates in negotiations with the prospect.

◆ *State Registration*—The charity must be in full compliance with state and federal law when issuing gift annuities.

◆ *Asset Management*—Donors trust charities to invest the assets used for gift annuities prudently. Charities must develop an appropriate investment strategy that is in compliance with federal and state regulations and protects the interests of the charity and the payment beneficiaries of the annuities.

Due to the complexity of the state regulations and the lack of internal expertise, even the largest charities typically outsource one or more of these asset management and administration functions.

Options to Issue Charitable Gift Annuities

There are five options that we typically recommend organizations consider when debating whether to directly offer gift annuities or their equivalent to your constituents.

◆ *Option 1:* Set Up and Manage Your Own Gift Annuity Program—The most traditional approach is for your organization to set up and manage its own gift annuity program. It would entail registration with your home state (if registration is required), establishment of reserve accounts, creation of asset management and administration policies and procedures, purchase of software, and staff training.

◆ *Option 2:* Set Up Your Own Gift Annuity Program and Hire an Outside Firm for Outside Management and/or Administration—The second option is a hybrid of the first; it removes the most onerous requirements by hiring a third party to provide asset management and administration. It still requires registration, purchase of software, and staff training. An outside firm is responsible for the establishment of reserve accounts and creation of asset management and administration policies and procedures. Among the vendors offering this type of service for a smaller program, you can expect a minimum fee of eighty basis points or $10,000 per year, whichever is more. In the early years this is a high-cost option, but over time would provide more flexibility and control over the program.

◆ *Option 3:* Set Up Your Own Gift Annuity Program, Hire an Outside Firm for Outside Management and/or Administration and Reinsure Some or All Risk—This option is the same as Option 2, but instead of taking on the risk associated with individual gift annuity contracts, you would purchase a policy of reinsurance on most or all of the gift annuities issued and transfer that risk to the insurance company. This reinsurance would limit the risks of starting a gift annuity program as it takes on the burden of making payments. Generally, it will cost between 60 and 75 percent of the original gift amount to purchase a policy of reinsurance, but it does release the remaining funds immediately. It also reduces the required reserves by an equivalent amount in many regulating states.

◆ *Option 4:* Use an Outside Charity to Issue Gift Annuities on Your Behalf—Rather than taking the many steps required to set up your own gift annuity program, you may instead rely upon another charity to issue gift annuities for your benefit. Since your organization would not be offering your own gift annuities, it would eliminate the requirements of such registration. You would still want to maintain planned giving software and train development staff on gift annuities so as not to be completely reliant on the issuing charity in your dealings with prospects interested in gift annuities. You would collect the basic donor information [name(s), date(s) of birth, gift amount and composition]. Once the gift is completed, the issuing charity prepares and provides the final calculations, the contract, gift summary, and the donor letter. They would also handle all investment and administrative responsibilities, including the distributions and form 1099-R, until the gift annuity contract terminates, at which time the distribution to your charity takes place. Because you are not the issuing charity, you take on no risk but have no control over the investment of the gift annuity reserves or setting gift annuity policies. If the gift annuity is depleted, there would be no final distribution.

◆ *Option 5:* Utilize Commercial Annuities Instead of Issuing Gift Annuities—Rather than issue gift annuities at all, it is possible to transfer the risk (and potential upside) to a commercial annuity company. Using this approach, instead of offering gift annuities or using a third-party charity, you would help the donor to compare quotes for commercial annuities paying the payment beneficiaries the same amount as an equivalent CGA for persons of that age. The donor would purchase the annuity AND make a gift of the difference between the cost of the commercial annuity and the original amount they planned to use to fund the gift annuity. For example, if a donor planned to set up a $100,000 gift annuity paying $7,000 per year, the donor should be able to go into the market and purchase a $7,000 per year commercial annuity for about $70,000. The donor would then make a gift of the remaining $30,000 to your organization outright. All of the risk has been transferred to the commercial annuity provider and you have use of the funds immediately. This amount is obviously less than the predicted residuum of 50 percent of the original gift amount, but it is in current dollars. Unfortunately, it also eliminates the possibility of your organization benefiting from a strong investment market during the time of the contract.

Pooled Income Funds

A pooled income fund (PIF) is a gift plan that allows donors to provide payments to themselves or others for life while they also make a generous gift to charity. It can be thought of as a "charitable mutual fund." PIF gifts can be established during live or through a will to benefit others. Gifts of cash or securities from multiple donors are combined, invested, and managed together in one common fund. The fund assigns "units" to the gift based on the total value of the fund. Each quarter the fund pays payment beneficiaries their proportional shares of net income based on the number of units assigned to the original gift.

When the payment beneficiary of a unit in the fund dies, the principal attributable to that unit is withdrawn from the fund and paid to your organization to be used for the purpose the donor specified when the gift was made. Distributions from a Pooled Income Fund can be for one or more lives and will fluctuate depending on the fund's investment performance and interest rates.

The donor will receive an income tax charitable deduction based on the fair market value of the assets contributed to the fund less the present value of the net income interest retained. If appreciated securities are contributed, the donor will avoid capital gains tax on the sale of those assets. The distributions will be taxable at ordinary income rates in the hands of the payment beneficiaries.

Pooled income funds typically appeal to individuals who wish to make a charitable gift and receive only net income in return. A PIF can provide portfolio diversification, but it cannot be relied upon to create a predictable income stream.

There are several types of pooled income funds, with names reflecting how the pool is invested:

◆ Growth Pooled Income Fund. The donor wants a stream of income that can grow over time by investing in growth investments. Early distributions tend to be small as the fund does not produce a great amount of investment income. Later, as the value of the units grows, the net income from those units will theoretically increase.

◆ Balanced or "Growth and Income" Pooled Income Fund. Your donor wants a stream of income that is stable but will also grow over time. The pool is invested in a fairly even mix of income producing investments and growth investments. This produces some income now, and then, as assets grow, increased income later.

◆ Standard Pooled Income Fund. Your client wants the maximum amount of income, so the fund is invested almost completely in income producing assets with very little potential for growth.

In the current low-interest-rate, low-inflation environment, coupled with a preference for total return investing, pooled income funds have largely fallen out of favor. Forming a new fund is rare and many nonprofits are closing their pooled funds as the last participants pass away.

It is possible for a pooled income fund to treat realized gains as income if the trust document allows it. In such cases, the fund can be invested for total return and still produce higher levels of distributions. It is a clever way to use a growth pooled income fund to produce income more in line with a standard pooled income fund. To amend an existing pooled fund to meet these criteria, all existing donors would have to approve it. Since it's hard to obtain 100 percent approval for larger funds, and it is not worth the effort for smaller funds, very few funds are converted. With the waning interest in new pooled funds, there are very few of these "total return" pooled income funds in existence. While it is possible to create a new pooled income fund based on this model, most organizations have elected to encourage charitable gift annuities or charitable remainder trusts instead.

If your organization does not offer a total return pooled income fund, it may be a worthwhile investment to open one, as it is an effective tool for individuals desiring payments with a hedge against inflation (that could grow over time) but whose gifts will not be large enough to form a charitable remainder trust. The only other option for these donors is to set up a series of flexible payment gift annuities and elect to start payments in a "laddered" sequence, thereby adding payments when needed. But this is a complex strategy compared to a simple pooled income fund gift.

Charitable Remainder Trusts

Transferring assets to a charitable remainder trust (CRT) is an ideal way to provide payment beneficiaries with fixed, variable, or deferred distributions for life or for up to twenty years while also supporting their favorite charities. Similar to a charitable gift annuity, donors can benefit from an immediate income tax charitable deduction for a portion of the funding amount and beneficial tax treatment of the distributions. When funded with appreciated property (which can include real estate and business interests), a portion of the capital gain associated with those assets is paid over the life of the trust or avoided altogether. CRTs can be established by the donor during life or by will.

At inception, all charitable remainder trusts must have a charitable deduction (charitable remainder value) of at least 10 percent of the funding amount. If a trust does not meet this test, it becomes a taxable trust rather than tax-exempt trust.

Charitable Remainder Unitrust

A charitable remainder unitrust (CRUT or unitrust) is a gift plan that allows a donor or donors to provide payments back to themselves or others while making a gift to charity. The payments may continue for the lifetimes of the beneficiaries named by the donor, a fixed term of not more than twenty years, or a combination of the two.

To establish a CRUT an attorney would draft the document and the assets are irrevocably transferred to the trustee of the trust (e.g. a bank trust department or a financial firm). Funding assets are typically cash, securities, or real estate to a trustee that the donor chooses.

During the unitrust's term, the trustee invests its assets and distributes a fixed percentage of the unitrust's value each year, as revalued annually, to the payment beneficiaries. If the unitrust's value goes up from one year to the next, its payout increases proportionately. Similarly, if the unitrust's value goes down, the amount it distributes goes down. For this reason, it may be to the donor's advantage to choose a relatively low payout percentage so that the unitrust assets can grow, which in turn will allow the unitrust's yearly payments to grow. Payments must be between 5 percent and 50 percent of the trust's annual value and are made out of trust income, or trust principal if income is not adequate. Payments may be made annually, semiannually, or quarterly.

> **Charitable Gift Annuities Are the Poor Man's Charitable Remainder Trust**
>
> Many donors over the years have used CGAs to great advantage to not only secure a steady stream of payments for themselves during retirement, but to also ensure that their favorite charity will be the beneficiary of a portion of their estate. Brian and I have met several people who, once they experienced the secure payments from one CGA, went on to set up several more. Each new gift annuity would add to their distributions, thereby increasing their "income" in retirement. It is similar to what these donors were doing in laddering their Certificates of Deposit, and often served as a replacement for CDs. As their CDs would come due and ready for renewal, we would get a call to do "another one of those gifts." For donors of more modest means, it allowed them to set up a payment stream in retirement that would increase each year, much like a charitable remainder unitrust, but they could start it with $10,000, instead of the $100,000 to $1 million minimum often required for trusts.
>
> —Robert
>
>  stories from the real world

When the unitrust term ends, the unitrust's principal passes to your charity to be used for the purpose designated by the donor. Since the trust is revalued annually, the donor may add funds to this trust. The donor qualifies for a federal income tax deduction for a portion of the value of the assets used to fund the unitrust.

The most common uses for CRUTs in charitable planning are to provide increased retirement income for younger retirees, wealth replacement to children when making charitable gifts, and in some cases to help pay for college education, as noted in *Getting Started in Charitable Gift Planning*.

Charitable Remainder Annuity Trust

A charitable remainder annuity trust (CRAT or annuity trust) is a gift plan that allows a donor or donors to provide fixed payments to themselves or others while making a gift to your organization. The payments may continue for the lifetimes of the beneficiaries the donor names, a fixed term of not more than twenty years, or a combination of the two. To establish an annuity trust, an attorney drafts the document and then the donor transfers assets—usually cash or securities—to a trustee chosen by the donor. The trustee then invests the trust assets and each year distributes a fixed dollar amount to the named payment beneficiaries.

The payments must be between 5 percent and 50 percent of the trust's initial value and paid from trust income, or trust principal if the income is not adequate. Payments continue until the trust term ends or until the unlikely event that the trust distributes all its assets. Payments may be made annually, semiannually, or quarterly. When the trust term ends, the trust's principal passes to your charity to be used for the purpose that the donor had designated. Since the annuity trust pays a fixed income, no additional funds can be added to this type of trust. The donor qualifies for a federal income tax deduction for a portion of the value of the assets transferred to establish the annuity trust. However, to qualify for this deduction, the CRAT must meet the 5 percent probability test. It requires all charitable remainder annuity trusts have less than a 5 percent chance of corpus exhaustion. If a CRAT fails the 5 percent test, no deduction is allowed.

The most common uses for CRATs in charitable planning are to provide increased retirement income for older retirees, or providing income to an elderly parent or friend, as noted in *Getting Started in Charitable Gift Planning*.

Net Income Unitrust

A net income charitable remainder unitrust (NICRUT) is a gift plan that allows a donor or donors to provide the lesser of net income or a set percentage of NICRUT assets each year for themselves or others while making a gift to your charity. The payments may continue for the lifetimes of the beneficiaries that are named, a fixed term of not more than twenty years, or a combination of the two. The assets transferred irrevocably are usually cash, securities, or real estate and are then invested by a trustee chosen by the donor.

During the NICRUT's term, the trustee will distribute a fixed percentage payment to the named income beneficiaries of between 5 and 50 percent of the NICRUT's value as revalued annually, or its net income, whichever is less. Payments are made annually, semiannually, or quarterly. If the NICRUT's value goes up from one year to the next, its payout increases proportionately. However, if the NICRUT earns less net income during a given year than the fixed percentage it is supposed to distribute, the unitrust distributes only what it earned. This "net income" feature guarantees that trust principal is never invaded to make a distribution. If the NICRUT's value goes down from one year to the next, the amount it distributes also goes down. For this reason, it may be to the donor's advantage to choose a relatively low payout percentage so the NICRUT assets can grow, which in turn allows the NICRUT's yearly payments to grow.

When the NICRUT's term ends, the principal passes to your charity to be used for the donors' intended purpose. Since the NICRUT is revalued annually, additional assets can be added to this type of trust. The assets transferred into the NICRUT will qualify for a federal income tax deduction equal to a portion of the value of the assets transferred to establish the trust.

Net Income with Makeup Unitrust

A charitable remainder unitrust with a makeup provision (NIMCRUT) is a NICRUT that includes a payment makeup provision. If the NIMCRUT earns less net income during a given year than the fixed percentage it is supposed to distribute, the trustee distributes only what it earned, or net income. This "net income" feature guarantees that NIMCRUT principal is never invaded to make a distribution. If in a subsequent year the NIMCRUT earns more than the fixed percentage, the NIMCRUT will make up its earlier shortfall to the extent that its net income exceeds its fixed percentage.

NICRUTs and NIMCRUTs are used less often since the advent of the Flip Unitrust. But if your donors are looking for income-only to maximize what is left for your charity from their gift, then these options may make sense.

Flip CRUT

A flip charitable remainder unitrust (flip CRUT) is a NICRUT or NIMCRUT with a provision that can cause the trust to become a CRUT upon the occurrence of a "triggering event" outside the control of the donor.

The method used to determine the amount of each year's payments depends on whether the payments are made before or after the trust "flips" its method of payment. During the preflip period, the trustee pays the beneficiaries either a fixed percentage of between 5 percent and 50 percent of the flip unitrust's value, as revalued annually, or its net income, whichever is less. This "net income" feature guarantees that the trust principal is not invaded to make a distribution during the preflip period. If the flip unitrust earns more than the fixed percentage during a later year within the preflip period, and the flip unitrust includes the makeup provision, the flip unitrust will make up its earlier shortfall to the extent that its net income exceeds its fixed percentage.

After the year of the occurrence of the "triggering event," which causes the "flip," the trustee pays the beneficiaries the unitrust's fixed percentage, regardless of the net income earned by the trust.

The triggering event is specified in the flip unitrust instrument. There are several allowable triggering events that will work including the sale of unmarketable assets such as real estate or closely-held stock, the arrival of a specific date, such as December 31, 2015, or a single event whose occurrence is not within the control of the trustee, donor or any other person, including the marriage, divorce, or death of a specific person, or the birth of a specific person's child.

The payment characteristics of a flip unitrust make it an especially useful vehicle for gifts of unmarketable assets that are expected to be sold once the trustee finds a buyer who is willing to pay a fair price. Prior to the flip in payment methods, the flip unitrust is obligated to distribute no more than its net income giving the trustee as much time as necessary to find a buyer. After the unmarketable assets are sold, the flip unitrust flips to paying its stated percentage regardless of its net income.

The most common uses for flip trusts in charitable planning are to provide future retirement distributions for younger donors and to help pay for college, as noted in *Getting Started in Charitable Gift Planning.*

To Recap

◆ Charitable gift annuities are a great way for donors to meet personal planning needs, such as increased retirement income or support for an elderly loved one, while also supporting your organization. Payments can start immediately, be deferred to the future, or compressed to meet personal planning needs.

◆ Charitable gift annuities are highly regulated, requiring compliance with regulations in both your organization's home state and the donor's state of domicile.

◆ Pooled income funds provide shared income, much like a charitable mutual fund, but have fallen out of favor due to low interest rates.

◆ Charitable remainder trusts are the workhorse of the Stage II gift planning program, offering fixed or variable income starting now or in the future to meet the personal planning objectives of your donors. However, due to the relatively high minimum investment, they make up only a small portion of gift planning revenue.

Chapter Three

Gifts That Maximize Inheritance

IN THIS CHAPTER

···→ Using a charitable lead trust to support a cause while assuring inheritance

···→ Allowing donors to witness outcomes of gifts and assure inheritance

···→ Providing for your cause now with donors or heirs receiving the assets back later

···→ Using wealth replacement trusts to assure future gifts and inheritance

For organizations which have developed Stages I and II, the Stage III donor-focused gift planning program provides for the full integration of donors' personal planning goals with their tax, estate, and financial planning, particularly their desire to maximize the inheritance to heirs. All of the tools of the gift planner are put to use, in collaboration with donors' advisors, to maximize personal planning and philanthropic goals. Stage III includes values-based estate planning that goes beyond the normal purview of charities, but, when it works, results in the largest gifts donors can make. Only a few nonprofits will ever offer a comprehensive Stage III program.

In this chapter, we describe variations on five charitable giving tools. The first of these tools, the charitable lead trust, offers four options depending upon the goals and objectives of your donors. What makes the lead trust unique is that the distributions during the trust term go to the nonprofit and the principal is returned to either the donor or the donor's family. The fifth tool, commonly referred to as the wealth replacement charitable remainder trust, makes payments to the donor for the purpose of funding a life insurance policy. When the trust ends, the life insurance policy pays its proceeds to heirs while the trust principal benefits your organization.

Charitable Lead Trust

A charitable lead trust (CLT) is essentially a charitable remainder trust in reverse. Your organization receives a payment stream (the payment interest), then, at the end of the specified trust term, which can be for a term of years, for the lifetime of the donor, or for the lifetimes of the donor and the donor's spouse, any income and principal remaining in the CLT (the remainder interest) can revert back to the donor (grantor CLT) or pass to other noncharitable beneficiaries named in the trust (nongrantor CLT). CLTs can make fixed payments to your charity, the charitable lead annuity trust (CLAT), or variable payments based upon the trust balance on the valuation date, known as a charitable lead unitrust (CLUT).

Using a CLT is an effective way to provide immediate support to your organization while passing assets to children or grandchildren at reduced gift and estate tax cost. Coupled with other complex estate planning techniques, the charitable lead trust provides the most benefit if the donor expects to be subject to estate tax. If the property contributed to the CLT appreciates at a greater rate than the amount paid to your organization each year, all appreciation remaining in the trust will pass free of gift and estate tax to the remainder beneficiaries. It is for this reason that CLTs can be used to leverage transfer tax exemption amounts in a way that allows reduced or tax-free transfer of wealth to children or grandchildren.

Whether a donor chooses to make their gift through a grantor or a nongrantor CLT, they will get an unlimited gift tax charitable deduction for the charitable lead interest. With a carefully determined trust term and charitable payout rate, the donor can reduce or avoid gift tax on the value of the trust remainder interest designated for their beneficiaries while also lowering the estate and gift tax cost of passing assets to heirs. Any appreciation within the trust during the trust term will pass free of gift or estate tax to the donor's beneficiaries when the trust terminates. This makes a lead trust a particularly good vehicle to transfer value to beneficiaries when a future need arises, such as when a child graduates from college.

Nongrantor Charitable Lead Annuity Trust

A nongrantor CLAT is a gift plan that allows a donor to transfer assets to family members at reduced tax cost while making a gift to your organization.

To establish a CLAT, an attorney drafts the documents and then the assets are irrevocably transferred to the trustee of the trust (e.g., a bank trust department or financial firm). Funding assets are usually cash or securities. Because the CLAT is a taxable trust, it is best to fund it with assets that are not appreciated. As the hope is to pass the appreciation on donated assets to heirs, ideally the assets used to fund the trust will be assets that have significant growth potential.

The CLAT Advantage

I recently worked with a significant donor who expressed an interest in passing as much of his estate as he could to his heirs. He was about to sell his closely-held business and wanted to avoid gift and estate tax. We modeled a CLAT to be funded with $20 million of company stock. Because the company would soon be sold, the donor estimated a 40 percent increase in the value of the CLAT assets in the year following the creation of the trust followed by 7 percent growth each year after that. Over its twenty-year term, the CLAT would pay the organization over $1 million per year, with nearly $45 million benefiting heirs free of gift and estate tax when the trust ended. This compared with just under $35 million that would have gone to heirs if the donor had not set up a CLAT. It is one of the rare cases where the donor's family and the charity are both better off financially because a charitable gift is made.

—Brian

stories from
the real world

During the CLAT's term, the trustee invests the trust's assets and provides a fixed dollar amount each year to your organization. These payments are used for the charitable purpose that the donor chose and continue until the trust term ends or the highly unlikely event that the trust distributes all its assets. The trust's term may be for a specific number of years (ten to twenty is common), one or more lifetimes, or a combination of the two. The payments are made out of trust income, or trust principal if the trust income is not adequate. If the trust income during a given year exceeds the annual charitable payment, the trust pays income tax on the excess.

When the CLAT term ends, the trust distributes all of its accumulated assets to family members or other beneficiaries named by the donor.

The CLAT is treated as a separate tax-paying entity subject to the income tax rules associated with trusts. All income and expenses are reported on a separate, fiduciary income tax return—they do not flow through the donor, and no income tax deduction is allowed to the donor, although the trust itself can deduct its annual payments to the charity. A CLAT can be created during the donor's lifetime or through the will.

Nongrantor Charitable Lead Unitrust

A nongrantor charitable lead unitrust (CLUT) is very similar to a CLAT, but instead of the trust making fixed payments to your organization each year, payments vary based on the value of the assets in the trust on the trust valuation date. Since the CLUT is valued annually, the donor can add funds to the unitrust at any time. If the CLUT's value goes up from one year to the next, its payout to your organization increases proportionately. Likewise, if the CLUT's value goes down, the amount it donates also goes down. These payments are used for the charitable purpose the donor chose and continue until the trust term ends or the highly unlikely event that the trust distributes all its assets.

Because of the variability of payments, the CLAT is generally preferred to the CLUT when used to reduce or avoid gift and estate tax on transfers to the donor's children. The variable payments could provide insufficient distributions to your organization from the CLUT to zero-out any gift/estate tax which might otherwise be due. However, when assets are passed to the donor's grandchildren, the CLUT may be the preferred vehicle to help avoid the generation-skipping tax. While the variability of payments is still an issue, when assets are passed to grandchildren, the generation-skipping tax also comes into play. When seeking to avoid the generation-skipping tax, a CLUT is preferred.

Grantor Charitable Lead Annuity Trust

A grantor charitable lead annuity trust (GCLAT) is a gift plan that allows your donor to transfer assets to family members at reduced tax cost while making a gift to your organization. Unlike the regular CLAT, the donor or grantor of a GCLAT is eligible to claim an income tax charitable deduction when the trust is created.

The term "grantor" in the CLT description refers to the "grantor trust rules" set forth in sections 671-679 of the Internal Revenue Code. If a trust includes any one of the provisions set forth in those rules, the individual who creates the trust is treated as the "owner" of the trust's income interest for income tax purposes. Many types of trusts fall into the "grantor trust" category, including revocable living trusts discussed in Chapter One that are often used in estate planning.

Because the donor/grantor is considered the owner of the CLT assets, all trust income and expenses pass through to the donor's income tax return and the donor can take an immediate income tax charitable deduction for the value of the payments to your organization from the GCLAT. Minimizing income taxes through an immediate income tax charitable deduction is the primary motive for creating a grantor lead trust. As a result, a grantor lead trust must be funded during life.

Grantor Charitable Lead Unitrust

A grantor charitable lead unitrust (GCLUT) is similar to the GCLAT, except that the GCLUT provides payments to your organization each year based on a fixed percentage of the GCLUT's current value.

On rare occasions, a grantor who has very rapidly appreciating property may use that property to create a GCLUT that will make large distributions to your organization during its term and return the remaining assets to the grantor, who may then create another GCLUT. This structure is used when:

◆ The grantor needs a large income tax deduction in a high-earning year;

◆ The grantor has special, perhaps high-income-producing assets that the donor wishes to have returned; and

◆ The grantor anticipates having a lower marginal income tax rate during the trust term.

Wealth Replacement Charitable Remainder Trust

A wealth replacement trust (WRT) is simply a charitable remainder trust (discussed in Chapter Two) paired with a life insurance policy. This mechanism allows your donor to make a gift to your organization and "replace" the wealth put into that trust with the proceeds of a life insurance policy. Because the life insurance proceeds pass to the donor's heirs tax free, it can save on income, gift, and estate taxes.

To create a WRT, the donor sets up a CRUT or CRAT with a payout rate high enough to cover the premiums on a life insurance policy with the same death benefit as the amount placed in the WRT. The donor then purchases a life insurance policy held inside of another trust, known as an irrevocable life insurance trust (ILIT) naming the heirs as beneficiaries. Because the trust is a separate entity from the insured's estate, the life insurance is not a part of the donor's estate and, therefore, not subject to estate tax.

Also, life insurance death benefits are not subject to income tax. In cases where the estate would be subject to estate tax, the proper use of an ILIT will enable the heirs to receive the death benefit free and clear of estate and income taxes and allow the donor to make a significant gift without disinheriting children or grandchildren.

To Recap

◆ For high-net-worth individuals who wish to maximize the inheritance for heirs and support your organization, it is possible to partially or completely avoid estate tax using charitable giving tools.

◆ A nongrantor charitable lead trust allows a donor to provide immediate support for your organization and to witness the outcome of the gift during the donor's lifetime, while at the same time maximizing the inheritance of a loved one—particularly in times of low discount rates.

◆ A grantor charitable lead trust allows a donor to provide immediate support for your organization while either maximizing the inheritance of a loved one or receiving the assets back at a later time. The donor has the added benefit of an income tax charitable deduction at the time of the gift, but will incur income tax during the term of the trust.

◆ A wealth replacement trust allows a donor to replace the amount of the gift to your organization so that the donor's heirs can receive the same, or perhaps even a greater benefit.

Chapter Four

Gifts of Complex Assets

IN THIS CHAPTER

- ---→ Encouraging gifts of stock and appreciated securities

- ---→ Developing gifts of business interests

- ---→ Be aware of gifts of life insurance

- ---→ Uncovering gifts of real estate and tangible personal property

Less than five percent of all assets are held in the form of cash. This means if you only ask your donors for gifts of cash, you are potentially leaving 95 percent of their giving potential on the table.

More importantly, you are encouraging gifts from their current income rather than gifts from their larger pool of assets. Gifts of complex assets can produce some of the largest gifts that your organization will ever receive, but without planning they can also cost time and effort with little result.

The best approach is to recognize that each case is different and that you must practice due diligence before agreeing to accept a complex-asset gift. Complex-asset gifts are the last piece needed to build your Stage III donor-focused gift planning program, or what we refer to as a philanthropic planning program.

If your organization does not have a gift acceptance policy be sure to review **Chapter Six** and work to adopt one so that you have some standards and guidance for gifts of complex assets. The simpler gifts, such as stock, bonds, and life insurance are quickly accepted by most organizations. Gifts of real estate and tangible personal property can be more challenging, but an effective checklist will help you determine if the gift is worth pursuing.

We espouse the basic idea that when approached with a complex-asset gift, the answer is "yes" until it is "no." By that, we mean you should explore each gift offered, using your policies and procedures, until you discover a reason not to accept it. But always keep in mind that it is far better to walk away from an issue that poses risk to your organization beyond the value of the prospective gift than to be captivated by the initial excitement of the offer.

Stock and Appreciated Securities

The most common of all gifts of complex assets are transfers to charity of publicly traded stocks, bonds, and mutual funds. To encourage charitable giving, federal law allows capital gains tax avoidance to donors when these assets have been held "long term" (i.e., more than one year). A donor of those assets will be able to claim an income tax charitable deduction for the fair market value of the asset on the date of the contribution and will not have to recognize capital gain on the disposition of the assets.

Depending on how your donor holds their securities, there are rules that determine the date on which the gift to charity is complete.

Securities Held by a Stockbroker or Banker

For securities held by a donor's stockbroker or banker, the securities typically will arrive most easily and efficiently through a depository trust company (DTC) transfer. The gift will be deemed complete when the securities arrive in your organization's account. To complete this gift, the donor will need your organization's account name, routing and account numbers, and tax identification number.

Securities Held in Certificate Form

How to "Accept" a Gift You Cannot Accept

Just because your organization is not able to accept a complex-asset gift does not mean that you need to turn it down. You may engage a third-party charity that specializes in complex-asset gifts to accept the gift on your behalf, liquidate it, and send you the proceeds less a fee. This is done regularly for automobile and boat donations. For large, complex assets, we often partner with the Dechomai Foundation in Jacksonville, Florida, and local community foundations, which have the resources to assist with these types of gifts. Your organization takes on no liability and outsources the difficulty of liquidation of the asset, but you still meet the planning objectives of your donor while also retaining the vast majority of the proceeds from the donated asset when it is sold by the third party.

 practical tip

---

For gifts of stock held in certificate form, your donor can mail the certificates, hand-deliver the certificates, or send the certificates using non-US Postal Service delivery services, such as FedEx or United Parcel Service. Each can result in a different date of gift for valuation and tax reporting purposes.

◆ *Postal Delivery:* When stock certificates are put in the mail, the donor should mail the certificates in one envelope and mail executed stock powers (which transfer ownership of the shares to your organization) in a separate envelope. If the shares and stock powers are mailed in the same envelope, it is much like sending cash through the mail, as someone intercepting the envelope can sell the shares using the stock power. The date of the gift will be the later postmark date on the envelope containing the stock power or the envelope containing the certificates. Note that the donor should never endorse the certificates and have them delivered; anyone could steal them and liquidate them.

◆ *Hand Delivery:* If the donor hand-delivers the certificates to your organization, the date of gift is the date of delivery. Ideally, the donor will not endorse the certificates and will deliver the certificates and executed stock powers. This ensures that the certificates are not accidentally endorsed incorrectly.

◆ *Delivery by a Non-US Postal Service Carrier:* As with gifts placed in the mail, when a donor sends certificates through a delivery service, the donor should send unendorsed certificates and stock powers in separate envelopes to ensure that they are not stolen. In such cases, the date of gift is the later date the certificates and stock power are *received* by your organization.

If the donor intends to make a gift at or near year-end, they will want to be sure the gift arrives in the taxable year intended. Even though it may seem counterintuitive, the donor is typically best served by sending the unendorsed certificates and stock powers via the US Postal Service (with some type of tracking attached), as the date of gift will be the date postmarked rather than risk a delivery company failing to complete a delivery before year-end.

Securities Held in Book Form

For gifts of stock held in book form (i.e., where the ownership of the stock is recorded on the books of the issuing corporation), your donor will need to contact the corporation and instruct it to transfer ownership of the stock to your organization. The date of the gift will be the date on which the stock is transferred into the charity's name. This process can be lengthy and its timing somewhat unpredictable, so the donor should initiate the transfer process several weeks or, better yet, months before the end of the tax year.

The IRS values stock gifts by taking the average or "mean" of the day's high and low price for the stock and multiplying that value by the number of shares received on the date of gift. If the gift is received on a weekend, holiday, or day on which the stock was not traded, an average of the mean values on the preceding and succeeding business days will be used. The value of a mutual fund share is its public redemption price on the day it reached your organization's account or was reissued in your organization's name.

Business Interests

Gifts of privately owned business interests, such as stock in closely-held corporations, S corporations, or professional partnerships, can be used for philanthropy while also assisting donors with succession planning or passing the business to children. Often, such interests are part of a family business or other small business created with a modest number of other shareholders. These interests frequently have a very low basis and significant appreciation.

The donor will receive an income tax charitable deduction for the full fair market value of the donated interests, with no capital gains tax liability for the transfer to your organization. However, unlike contributions of publicly traded stock, for which value is easily determined, closely-held stock and other nonpublicly traded interests are not readily valued. To determine the value, the donor must obtain a qualified appraisal at the donor's own expense. The donor will report the value of the gift on IRS Form 8283 (Noncash Charitable Contributions).

In some cases your donor may be able to use the interest to fund a gift plan that pays income for life, such as a charitable gift annuity, charitable remainder unitrust (in which case the income tax charitable deduction will be limited to the value of the charitable portion of the interest contributed), or a gift that lowers the gift/estate tax cost of passing a family business to the next generation. Keep in mind that gifts of business interests are complex, and different rules apply to different business types (C corporations versus S corporations for example).

Life Insurance

As noted, suggesting that your donor name your organization as a beneficiary of an existing life insurance policy is a useful way to make a legacy gift. But it is also possible for your donor to make an outright of life insurance to benefit your organization.

Gift of Life Insurance: Keep It or Liquidate It?

Once a gift of life insurance is completed to your organization, you need to determine if you should remain invested in the policy or liquidate it. For smaller organizations without sophisticated investment managers, the benefits of staying in the insurance policy may outweigh the higher costs and fees (commissions to brokers and investment management fees) associated with investing in life insurance. But for organizations with strong investment returns, liquidating the policy and reinvesting the proceeds may make more sense unless the insured has a health history that would suggest a life expectancy less than the standard life expectancy tables.

If your organization elects to hold donated policies, given the challenges with the insurance industry along with the variety of policies that exist, charities need to pay attention to the life insurance policies that they own to ensure that they are financially sound and continue to meet your needs over time.

important

Life insurance is an interest-rate-sensitive financial instrument designed to pay a benefit at an unknown point in time. The principal uses have been for income for a spouse and/or children, to pay debts, to pay for education for children or grandchildren, to provide special needs, to offer an additional source of cash in retirement, to create an estate, to fulfill business needs (e.g., buy/sell arrangements, assistance for the recruitment or loss of key employees, and deferred compensation), and wealth replacement (discussed in Chapter Three) or charitable giving.

When policy owners no longer need to insure against these risks, the question becomes, "What should I do with the policy?" As a general rule, term insurance policies are allowed to lapse, as they have no cash value associated with them to provide for other uses if the policy does not mature. However, permanent insurance, such as universal and whole life policies, accumulate cash tax free inside the policy (premiums minus mortality expenses and sales/administration expenses). This accumulated value can be used by your donor for personal planning needs or to make a charitable gift. Regardless of the type of life insurance, benefits are income tax free to beneficiaries. While this does not usually help charitable organizations, which are tax exempt, it can be tremendously helpful for family members.

Life insurance can be a wonderful giving tool in the right circumstance. For organizations without sophisticated investment management, it allows a donor to leverage their dollars into a much larger gift. It can also offer a guaranteed death benefit/gift that may be vital to the long-term survival of charities of modest means. When the policy is owned by your organization, it becomes an irrevocable gift and the annual premiums paid by the donor are deductible as additional charitable gifts. As noted earlier in the research of Russell James, irrevocable legacy gifts are increasingly important. With the increase in transfers outside of wills, legacy gifts will become harder to come by over time.

While life insurance has its place, it also has its pitfalls. It is rarely beneficial for a donor to purchase a new policy of permanent insurance and name the charity as owner and beneficiary. The organization should be able to invest the initial premium amount and the equivalent of premiums more efficiently than through an insurance policy. Universal insurance may not have a guaranteed death benefit and may result in an organization owing additional premiums which the donor is not willing to pay. If you plan to deal with insurance gifts, be sure to find an insurance professional to guide your efforts.

Real Estate

Gifts of real estate can provide substantial benefits for your organization while saving the donor thousands of dollars in income, estate, and capital gains taxes, all while removing burdensome maintenance, insurance, and real estate tax costs. Real estate frequently is the single largest asset owned by potential donors and can serve as a wonderful way to make a charitable gift. The donor will receive an income tax charitable deduction based on the fair market value of the property (or the charitable portion of gift in which there is a retained interest), and the donor will avoid and/or defer capital gains liability on the transfer provided the property has been owned for over one year. There are many gift options that your donors may consider depending on their circumstances and the real estate in their portfolios.

Gifts of real estate can be subject to risk. To accept gifts of real estate, your organization should develop a two-step process to evaluate real estate. The first step is an initial screening to gather essential information about the prospect, the property, and any proposed gift structures.

The preliminary review should be donor-friendly and help to eliminate properties with significant challenges or that your organization simply is not prepared to accept. In particular, liability for environmental contamination passes with the deed to a property. If your organization suspects any potential environmental concerns, a Phase I environmental assessment should be completed before moving to the second step.

If the property passes the preliminary review, the second step is to work collaboratively with your donor through a more detailed due diligence process. Due diligence should help ensure that your organization identifies any potential risks with the property and minimizes them. In some cases, it may make sense to use a third-party nonprofit or a supporting organization to accept the gift on your behalf and minimize your risk.

> **Educate the Potential Donor about Valuation Methodology *Before* the Transfer**
>
> Be sure to share the valuation methodology with potential donors before a transfer. We have witnessed many donors who refuse to ever give to an organization again because the valuation was lower than expected, even though this is entirely outside of the organization's control.
>
>
> important

Your organization should understand the donor's reasons for wanting to donate real estate and explain to the donor the due diligence you must undertake to ensure you can accept the property and convert it easily to proceeds that can be applied to the donor's charitable purposes.

Outright Gifts of Real Estate

All types of real estate may be given to support your organization. The most typical gifts will be a personal residence, a vacation home, or a rental property. More rarely a prospect will offer a farm or commercial property.

The type of real estate will impact the donor's income tax charitable deduction. A donor will be able to claim the full fair market value of the property as an income tax charitable deduction and generally avoid any capital gain associated with the property. For commercial or rental properties, there may be some depreciation recapture that results in some capital gains tax not being avoided.

Gifts of personal residences and vacation homes are rarely complicated and often will not require a great deal of due diligence compared to other types of properties. Again, your organization should be careful not to accept properties with environmental concerns or are otherwise unmarketable.

Sample Materials

Real Estate Screening Tool

Legal Owners of the Property:_____

Best Contact Address:_____

Best Phone Number: _____ Email:_____

Address/Location of Property to Be Donated:_____

Adjacent to Organization's Existing Properties: Y/N

Size of Property:_____

Current Use of Property:_____

Zoning of Property and Surrounding Properties:_____

Current Value of Property:_____

Listing Price (if currently on market):_____

Date of Acquisition:_____

Cost Basis (price paid plus improvements):_____

Mortgage or Debt Amount:_____

Environmental Concerns (underground or above-ground tanks, prior agricultural use, prior commercial use):_____

Why does the prospect want to donate the property at this time?_____

_____

Type of Gift (please circle): Outright   Retained Life Estate   Bargain Sale   Life-Income

Recommendation:

_____ Reject Property

_____ Continue with Due Diligence

Real Estate in Exchange for Lifetime Income

A donor can use real estate to make a gift in exchange for payments for life. Typically, these gifts use a flip charitable remainder trust as described in **Chapter Two.** The donor transfers the real estate to the trustee of the flip trust and claims a partial income tax charitable deduction. The trust then pays the net income from the trust to the payment beneficiary until the sale of the property. When the property sells, it triggers the "flip" and starting the following year, the trust pays out the stated payout percentage (typically 5 to 7 percent).

The flip trust protects the trustee from having to make full payments until after the property sells. However, it may be necessary for the donor to make an additional gift to the trust with cash or other marketable assets so that the trust has sufficient resources to maintain the property, pay property taxes, cover costs of the sale, pay the trustee, or meet other expenses of the trust.

In some states, it is also possible to offer a charitable gift annuity in exchange for real estate. Since a gift annuity is a contractual arrangement between your organization and the donor, the funding asset does not impact the transaction. Even so, if you accept real estate in exchange for a gift annuity, you will need to find other assets to include in your gift annuity reserve to protect your organization from risk while you sell the property. If you elect not to sell the property, those assets will be tied up for the life of the annuitant.

Many organizations that offer gift annuities in exchange for real estate will defer the start of payments one or two years, to help ensure that the property is sold before CGA payments begin, or will negotiate a lower rate than the American Council on Gift Annuities' recommended rate, since the proceeds likely will be reduced by costs and it will take time to sell the property. Ideally, your organization would do both, thereby ensuring that the donor's charitable purpose is not eroded by the costs of the gift vehicle involved.

Retained Life Estate

One of the most popular real estate gifts involves a gift of the remainder interest in a home while the donor retains the right to use it during life. The donor benefits from an income tax charitable deduction for the charitable portion now (in many cases over 70 percent of the value of the home and property), but otherwise nothing changes.

> ### Say, Is That a Partial Interest?
>
> Donors may own many types of real estate interests, including mineral interests. Mineral interests are the right to exploit, mine, or produce minerals lying beneath the surface of a property, such as oil, gas, coal, and ore. The owner cannot strip away the mineral interests (a partial interest) and donate them to your organization (and claim a deduction) if the owner has title to other rights in the property. But if the only rights the donor owns are the mineral rights, they are deductible when donated. The ownership of the mineral rights is an interest in real property, but once extracted, the minerals become personal property. Because mineral rights, water rights, view rights, and other rights are complicated, always confer with a real estate attorney who specializes in this area if you are offered an unusual real estate interest.
>
> **observation**

As the creator of a retained life estate, the donor irrevocably deeds the home (or farm) to your organization but retains the right to live in it for life, a term of years, or a combination of the two. While they retain the right to live on the property, they continue to be responsible for all routine expenses—maintenance fees, insurance, property taxes, repairs, etc. If they later decide to vacate the property, they may rent all or part of the property to someone else or sell the property in cooperation with your organization. When the retained life estate ends, your organization can then use the property or the proceeds from the sale of the property for the purpose designated by the donor.

Retained life estates are very popular with individuals who have no children and for vacation/seasonal homes. For example, if a married couple with no children plans to leave your organization their entire estate, they can deed over their home now and retain the right to live there for life. Nothing else changes for them, but they benefit from a large income tax charitable deduction to help reduce their current tax bill.

With the aging of the Leading Baby Boomer generation, we find they do not want to retire or vacation in the same locations as their parents. As a result, they are not interested in owning seasonal or vacation homes that their parents had purchased in locations such as Florida or Arizona. The parents, not wanting to burden their children with the liquidation of these homes upon their deaths, can donate the property to your nonprofit, retaining the right to use it for life. Not only does it provide them with a nice current income tax deduction, it also eliminates the need for heirs to liquidate the property after their death. It may even avoid the parents' estates from having to go through ancillary probate (i.e., probate in two states because property is owned in more than one jurisdiction).

Charitable Bargain Sale

If a donor wants to make a gift of real estate to your organization but needs some of the value out of the property, the donor can sell their property to your organization for a discounted price. Your organization will pay them in a lump sum or issue them an installment note for the cash portion and the donor will benefit from an income tax charitable deduction for, and avoid capital gains tax on, the charitable portion of the gift.

A bargain sale is executed using a simple gift agreement, coupled with a deed in the case of real estate. The typical donor wants to make a gift of property that is no longer used or do not want to maintain, but from which some cash would be beneficial—perhaps for a down payment on a retirement home, a child's educational expenses, or just a nest egg. Most often, bargain sales are used for real estate, but they can also be used in some cases for other types of property (e.g. artwork, antiques, and collectibles).

Tangible Personal Property

The Leading Baby Boomer generation has been focused on building collections most

---

The America's Cup: Famous Example of a Deed-of-Gift Transaction

One of the most famous deed-of-gift transactions involves the oldest trophy in sport—The America's Cup. After the schooner *America* defeated the English yachts in a race around the Isle of Wight in England in 1851, the Royal Yacht Squadron presented the trophy to the winning yacht. The "Auld Mug" as it is also known was renamed the America's Cup after the first winning yacht and was donated to the New York Yacht Club under the terms of the Deed of Gift, which made the cup available for perpetual international competition.

Any yacht club that meets the requirements specified in the original Deed of Gift has the right to challenge the yacht club that holds the Cup. If the challenging club wins the match, it gains stewardship of the cup. In 2013, with the Golden Gate Bridge and Alcatraz as the backdrop, Oracle Team USA defeated the Emirates Team New Zealand in a dramatic come-from-behind victory to successfully defend the cup. Down eight points to one, Oracle Team USA, skippered by Jimmy Spithill, won seven races to force a winner-take-all final race to win the regatta.

 **stories from the real world**

of their adult lives. From art to stamps, to antiques, to coins, to milk bottles, to baseball cards, all of these collectibles are treated as tangible personal property for tax purposes. Tangible personal property is any physical object that may be moved and is not permanently fixed to any real estate. When tangible personal property is sold, any gains attributable to the property are taxed at a higher rate than other capital gain property, making it an attractive asset to donate.

The most common gift of tangible personal property that your organization will be offered is art. Individuals may own paintings, sculptures, porcelain, artistic screens, scrimshaw, carvings, and other types of art. Generally, rare books, letters, and other written materials may be considered art.

In most circumstances, the donor completes a gift of tangible personal by making a physical transfer of the asset accompanied by a deed of gift.

Because gifts of tangible personal property, and particularly art, can be complicated, it is important to find experts to assist you when evaluating and accepting such assets, much like we suggest for real estate. But as you review potential gifts of tangible personal property, keep the following in mind:

◆ Gifts of a Fractional Interest: The Pension Protection Act of 2006 made substantial changes to the rules surrounding gifts of tangible personal property, especially since they relate to art. Under these rules, it is possible for donors to make gifts of fractional interests, but once the first fractional interest is donated, future fractional interests must be the lesser of the fair market value at the time of the original gift or at the date of the subsequent gift of a fractional interest. If the entire interest is not donated within ten years, then all previous deductions are recaptured. Finally, your nonprofit must have actual possession of the art for the same fraction of each year that it has ownership (10 percent interest equals 36.5 days of possession).

◆ Qualified Appraisal: When the income tax charitable deduction for tangible personal property exceeds $5,000, the donor must obtain a qualified appraisal and submit Form 8283. If your organization sells the property within three years, you must file Form 8282. This alerts the IRS if your sales price is substantially less than the claimed deduction. Because of this requirement, some donors will request that your organization hold donated tangible personal property more than three years after it is donated. They erroneously believe that by your holding the property, they will avoid IRS scrutiny. It is best not to assist even your most loyal donors with any efforts to commit tax fraud.

◆ Related Use: For your donor to claim a fair market value income tax charitable deduction when

---

Donor Turns Related-Use Lemons Into Lemonade!

I once worked with a museum of contemporary art and the donor wanted to make an art donation. The particular piece was considered "contemporary" and appraised at $5 million, after being purchased for $1 million several years earlier. Unfortunately, this particular museum had no standing collection, as contemporary art does not remain "contemporary" very long. Further, the donor anticipated the museum would sell the art and wanted to designate how the museum would use the proceeds. Unable to work around the related-use rule, the donor elected to have the piece sold at auction, which it did, for more than double the appraised value. The donor then made a donation of $5 million in other appreciated assets to help offset some of the taxes due on the gain resulting from the sale.

—Brian

stories from the real world

making a gift of tangible personal property, the donor must reasonably believe that your organization will use the donated object in a way that is related to your exempt purpose. If the object cannot be used for such a purpose, the donor's deduction is limited to cost basis. It does not matter if your organization holds the donated tangible personal property more than three years and thus does not have to file Form 8282. The two are not "related." Note, too, that gifts from estates are not subject to the related-use rule.

As with real estate, it is possible to use tangible personal property to fund gift annuities, charitable remainder trusts (typically the flip charitable remainder trust), and bargain sales. However, because a charitable remainder trust cannot use the tangible personal property for a related use, the income tax charitable deduction is substantially limited. For donors who want payments in return for gifts of tangible personal property, installment bargain sales and gift annuities are typically the best options.

IRA Charitable Rollover

For many individuals, the largest percentage of their net worth is tied up in retirement accounts. For those with assets in an Individual Retirement Account (IRA), it is possible to make lifetime gifts from the IRA (qualified charitable distributions) directly to your nonprofit using a provision known as the IRA Charitable Rollover. To qualify:

◆ The donor must be age 70½ or older at the time of gift.

◆ Transfers must be made directly from a traditional IRA account to your organization. Funds that are withdrawn by the donor and then contributed do not qualify as IRA Charitable Rollovers.

◆ Gifts from 401k, 403b, SEP, and other plans are not qualified charitable distributions.

◆ Gifts must be outright. Distributions to donor-advised funds or life-income arrangements such as charitable remainder trusts and charitable gift annuities are not allowed.

Qualified charitable distributions:

◆ Can total up to $100,000 per spouse per year

◆ Are not included in your donor's gross income for federal income tax purposes on the IRS Form 1040

◆ Do not qualify your donor for an income tax charitable deduction

◆ Count toward your donor's required minimum distribution (RMD) for the year from the IRA

The IRA Charitable Rollover is best for individuals who do not itemize deductions or are subject to income tax deduction phase outs. For most individuals with an IRA, it is usually better from a tax perspective to give your organization appreciated stock rather than complete an IRA Charitable Rollover, as the donor benefits from both an income tax charitable deduction and avoidance of capital gains tax. However, for some donors, particularly those who have large IRAs and will be required to take minimum distributions they do not need, an IRA Charitable Rollover will seem like a reasonable solution. As always, it is wise to advise your donors to consult with their own advisors when considering any type of gift arrangement.

To Recap

◆ Cash and stock make up less than 20 percent of the portfolio held by high-net-worth donors. When you limit yourself to accepting cash and stock, you leave 80 percent of potential gifts on the table.

◆ Many of the wealthiest, particularly among those born after 1946, are entrepreneurs who own businesses and need exit strategies to pass those businesses to purchasers or heirs. Charitable giving techniques can provide a tax-efficient way to make those transfers while supporting your organization.

◆ Life insurance policies with cash value can be used to make a charitable gift from an asset that is no longer needed for its intended purpose.

◆ If you properly manage the risks associated with real estate gifts, they can be an excellent way for your donors to make large gifts, particularly of second homes now or at death (through a retained life estate) or real estate investments they no longer want.

◆ Many Leading Baby Boomers have extensive collections that can make substantial gifts to your organization. Just be sure your donor understands the implications of the related-use rule when giving an asset not related to your charitable mission.

◆ The IRA Charitable Rollover provides donors age 70½ and older with an additional option to consider when making outright charitable gifts.

Chapter Five

Answers to Common Gift Planning Questions

IN THIS CHAPTER

◆ What is planned giving / gift planning?

◆ What is a charitable gift and when is it deductible?

◆ Understanding the common terms of gift planning

◆ What life events could provide gift planning opportunities?

Formerly known as planned giving and widely used as the term for the third leg of the individual-gifts fundraising stool (the other two legs are annual giving and major giving), planned giving should now be referred to as gift planning to better represent the new, donor-focused approach.

Planned giving was all about the charity and the gift vehicles, while gift planning focuses on donor needs and wishes. It is a process for integrating an individual's philanthropic goals into the overall tax, estate, and financial plan. It often involves a variety of flexible charitable giving vehicles that allow a donor to support charitable organizations with larger gifts than from current income.

Philanthropic planning is a new approach that goes even deeper into the process with donors, their families, and their professional advisors to meet their tax, financial, and estate planning goals while also crafting their legacy. Philanthropic planning uses all three stages of the gift planning program described in earlier chapters to help donors achieve their charitable goals. As noted in *Getting Started in Charitable Gift Planning*, it requires a strong partnership with donors' advisors and a real dedication to donor-focused outcomes. If your organization is only interested in "what's in it for us," it's not ready for a philanthropic planning program.

What Is a Charitable Contribution?

An irrevocable gift of money or other property made to a qualified charity, either during life or by will.

What Is a Charitable Deduction?

A contribution or a gift to a charity that is deemed tax deductible. There are several rules that apply depending on the type of charity supported and the type of gift that is given. Charitable deductions also vary according to the type of individual or organization that is making the gift.

◆ "Contributions or gifts to or for the use of" charities are deductible because they serve the public interest. A gift to a friend or family member is not deemed to serve the public interest and thus is not deductible. However, gifts for helping with relief efforts, education, medical services for the needy, social services, or religious organizations are deemed to benefit the greater public interest and are therefore deductible for income tax purposes.

◆ The gift must be made voluntarily. For instance, if the charitable contribution is required by a court of law, it is not made voluntarily.

◆ If a donor receives goods or services in return for a gift, a charitable deduction may still be allowable if the donor's gift was "in excess of any benefits received" from the charity. In general, the charitable deduction will equal the difference between what the donor contributed less what the donor received.

◆ Intangible religious benefits or a benefit such as the naming of a building generally do not reduce a donor's charitable deduction. Such benefits are deemed intangible, incidental, and of little or no value.

When Is a Gift Deductible?

The general rule for deducting charitable contributions is that a gift is deductible in the tax year when paid to or delivered to a charity. Pledges are promises to pay in the future and not deductible until payment or delivery occurs. When determining gift payment or delivery, the continued possession by the donor usually indicates that a tax deductible gift has not yet been made.

◆ Cash or check: If a gift is deductible when delivered to charity, to complete a charitable gift by check, a taxpayer may simply hand-deliver a check to the charity. There is a special "mailbox" rule for checks mailed to charity. That rule states that checks are deductible on the date of unconditional mailing or delivery via the US Postal Service, even though the final transfer to charity is not actually made until the check clears the banking institution. Therefore, so long as the check clears in the normal course of business, the charitable deduction will be allowable in the year the donor mailed the check. A postdated check is a promise to pay in the future and, thus, not deductible at time of delivery.

◆ Credit card: Gifts by credit card are deductible in the year when the charges are made on the card owner's account. Since credit card charges are normally immediately created by electronic debit on an account, the credit card gift is immediately deductible.

◆ Stocks: Stocks may be transferred by hand delivery, electronic delivery, or through the mail. For more details, see **Chapter Four.**

When Is It Better to Give Stock Rather than Cash?

While writing a check may be the simplest method to make a gift, it is often not the most tax-efficient gift. We have all cringed when a donor says to us that they just sold their stock to make a gift to our organization. We are grateful for their gift, but we could have assisted them in avoiding some tax with a little bit of planning. While donors are not particularly motivated by tax incentives to make charitable gifts, once they decide to make a gift, they DO want that gift to be as tax efficient as possible and are disappointed when they learn of inefficiency after the fact.

Gifts of cash and stock both provide an income tax charitable deduction for the face value of the gift. But donating appreciated stock can help your donor avoid the capital gains tax that would be paid if the donor sold the stock and gave your organization the proceeds. With most taxpayers paying capital gains at 20 percent, this can result in significant savings. The exception is the donor who is already claiming deductions of more than 30 percent of adjusted gross income, as in that case a gift of appreciated stock is no longer deductible while a gift of cash is deductible up to 50 percent of adjusted gross income.

Who Are the "Remaindermen" and Why Are They Helpful to Our Cause?

A remainderman or remainder beneficiary is an individual or organization that has a remainder interest in a trust or in an item of property. When your organization is named as the remainderman or remainder beneficiary of a charitable remainder trust, it receives the remaining assets when the other beneficiaries' interests end.

How Do You Get Your Donors to Include Your Organization in Their Will?

One of the simplest and perhaps the most beneficial gift that a donor can make is by making plans to include a provision for your organization through a will. As a fundraiser, you should identify the best legacy giving prospects, talk to them about legacy gifts, and market the concept as part of a comprehensive gift planning strategy. When loyal donors are asked why they have never included a charitable organization in their will or other estate planning documents, the typical answer is, "It never occurred to me and no one asked." Be sure you ask.

How Do You Get Your Donors to Include Your Organization as a Beneficiary of a 401(k)/403(b) or Other Retirement Plan?

When retirement plan assets are passed to anyone other than a surviving spouse, they can be subject to income and estate taxes in excess of 70 percent. When the same assets are passed to your organization, there is no tax due. Ask your donors to name your organization as the beneficiary of the retirement plan and leave other assets to children. The tax savings alone could result in more for children while making a larger charitable gift than they ever thought possible. Best of all, it is an easy way for a donor to make a testamentary gift. It does not require a lawyer, only the execution of a simple change of beneficiary form available from the retirement plan provider.

What Is a Complex Asset and Why Should I Care?

The donor-focused charitable gift planning approach requires charities to have the capacity to accept many types of assets as gifts from donors. Nearly 80 percent of assets held by individuals are in forms other than cash or appreciated stock. They include retirement accounts, real estate, closely held and family businesses, hedge funds and private equity, art and collectibles, and other personal property. The ability to accept these assets allows donors to start crafting their legacy today while making larger and more meaningful gifts with resources beyond the cash and stock on hand.

What Is Meant by the Term "Quid Pro Quo"?

"Quid pro quo" translates as, roughly, "this for that." In other words, the donor makes a gift and the charity transfers some goods, service, or benefit back to the donor. If a donor's gift exceeds $75 and there is a quid pro quo, then the charity is subject to reporting requirements. If the gift is $75 or more and goods or services are transferred from the charity to the donor, then a detailed receipt must be given to the donor. The receipt must show the value of the gift and the charity's good faith estimate of the goods and services provided to the donor.

Common benefits provided to donors by charities include admission to special events, dinners, gala auctions, education, raffle drawing prizes, and preferred seating. In each case, it is important to determine whether the donor's gift was "in excess of any benefits received" from the charity. If so, then a charitable deduction should be allowable for the difference. If not, it is likely that no charitable deduction is allowed.

For example, a donor contributes $200 to attend a special dinner event. In return, the donor is provided meals and benefits reasonably valued at $50. The donor is entitled to a charitable deduction equal to $150 because $150 is the difference between what was given versus what was received.

Auctions are frequently held by charities and some purchasers have mistakenly believed that their successful bids were deductible. However, since the individual receives the auction property, there is usually no deduction. But if the winning bid can be shown to be in excess of the fair market value of the item, that excess amount is deductible.

Several types of gifts do not result in deductions. For example, payment of tuition to an organization for your child or grandchild produces no deduction. The benefit of education for the child is equal to the tuition paid and there is no charitable gift. Also, the purchase of raffle tickets is generally not deductible because the chance to win a prize is deemed equal to the price of the raffle, i.e., no excess gift element. When preferred seating is offered to donors, the Tax Code states that only 80 percent of a donor's gift is deductible.

What Life Events Could Provide Gift Planning Opportunities?

Most donors do not wake up in the morning and decide, "Today would be a good day to change my estate planning" to include your organization. In reality, charitable gift planning occurs either in response to a solicitation by your organization (major gift or planned gift) or because the donor has undergone a significant life event that warrants changes to an existing plan (or creation of a first plan) and your organization is included. To be included, you need to be front of mind when the donor experiences one of these life events that prompt estate planning:

- ◆ Birth
- ◆ Marriage
- ◆ Divorce
- ◆ Graduation
- ◆ Accident and/or illness
- ◆ Death of spouse, domestic partner, or loved one
- ◆ Moving to another state
- ◆ Vacations
- ◆ Inheritance
- ◆ Job/career change

- Sale or transfer of family-owned business

- Addition or subtraction of major asset from holdings

- Sale/merger of a company in which the donor has major holdings

- Retirement

- Natural disasters

- Travel abroad

It is impossible for your organization to predict when these events may occur or if they will be the trigger for gift planning. It is important that you have a relationship with the donor so that when such an event occurs, your organization will be well positioned to suggest gift planning alternatives to meet both personal planning and charitable giving goals.

To Recap

- Gift planning is a process that integrates a donor's tax, estate, and financial planning with philanthropic goals.

- Just because a gift is put to a charitable purpose does not mean that it will be deductible for tax purposes.

- While donors are not particularly motivated by tax incentives to make charitable gifts, once they decide to make a gift, they want that gift to be as tax efficient as possible. Gifts of stock tend to be more efficient than gifts of cash.

- The best way to close beneficiary designations from wills and retirement plans is to consistently mention them when talking with and marketing to loyal donors to your organization.

- Complex assets are often overlooked for charitable gifts yet make up the vast majority of the holdings of most donors. By understanding and encouraging these gifts as part of your gift planning program, you will dramatically increase the fundraising results for your organization.

- Gift planning occurs in response to being asked, or in response to an important event in the life of the donor. By building a relationship and remaining in touch with your organization's donors, you increase the likelihood that you will be aware of one of these life events and be prepared to discuss gift planning at the appropriate moment.

Part Two

Tools to Help You Build Your Gift Planning Program

Building the core infrastructure for your gift planning program, identifying your gift planning prospects, segmenting your list, and crafting a plan for moving these prospects through your moves management process—this is the hands-on work of gift planning that requires you to proactively build relationships with identified prospects and to help them meet personal planning goals while supporting your nonprofit. Though it is often challenging, it is also the most rewarding part of gift planning work, as you get to work with people loyal to your cause who want to make a meaningful difference. The best days you have as a gift planner are the days you help prospects turn their philanthropic dreams into reality while also securing the future for their families.

In *Getting Started in Charitable Gift Planning,* we provided information on how to create a culture of philanthropy; performance goals; the roles of your staff, board, volunteers, and professional advisors; how to identify prospects and segment your list; conducting visits; and a broad overview of stewardship and marketing. In the next few chapters, we focus on some of the basic tools you will need to implement these steps for your organization.

Chapter Six

Infrastructure

IN THIS CHAPTER

- ···→ Crafting the internal case
- ···→ Developing gift counting and recognition policies
- ···→ Understanding best practices for gift acceptance policies and gift agreements
- ···→ Using an estate administration process to collect matured planned gifts

Many gift planning programs struggle because they are not committed long term. They never put in place the core elements of a strong, sustainable program. Instead, they "jump to the end" and offer Stage III, complex gift planning tools without building the proper infrastructure and program plan to support it. Over time, the program loses momentum or other priorities take its place, and the nonprofit stops actively pursuing it. Sound familiar? We've seen it happen over and over. The key to success is building your infrastructure one step at a time.

While we say that gift planning is easy, developing infrastructure may be the most difficult part. It starts with an internal case—which reminds senior management, staff, board, and donors about the importance of gift planning to the organization both today and long term. Without it, your program will start and stop. Donors will shy away from it.

Once a case has been developed, adopt a gift acceptance policy. It is incredibly difficult for an organization to turn down a gift—no matter how bad it may be for the organization—without a policy in place. Such a policy provides real cover when you are being pushed to accept a gift that could harm the cause down the road.

A policy on gift counting and recognition also protects a charity—in this case, from future arguments with donors. You should be able to clearly articulate what dollar value you will put on a gift and how you will recognize it *before* the donor makes a transfer. Waiting until the gift has been completed leads to unhappy donors and administrators. This is especially important with gifts using difficult-to-value assets or life insurance.

You will often find that these types of discussions are facilitated by the gift agreement process. When you require a gift agreement for multiyear, restricted, and complex gifts, it ensures that you ask these questions ahead of time, rather than after the gift has been completed.

The final piece of infrastructure for a strong gift planning program is an estate administration process. After all, there is little point in encouraging estate gifts if you never collect them!

The Internal Case

One of the first steps on the road to a successful gift planning program is drafting an internal case. The case should:

◆ Invoke the highest purpose of your organization's existence—it should include the mission and demonstrate how the fulfillment of your long-term mission will be strengthened through legacy and endowment gifts.

◆ Focus on the needs of your donors—how through legacy and endowment gifts your donors can be assured that their support will enhance the part of your mission that is most important to them, and that they can establish a meaningful and permanent legacy that meets your needs while also meeting their philanthropic objectives.

◆ Provide the rationale behind the request for legacy and endowment gifts.

◆ Identify a range of long-term resource needs and objectives.

◆ Serve as the springboard for creating a variety of communication and marketing efforts in support of your future and endowment giving program.

The case targets your internal audience, particularly your staff and volunteer board, to help change the organizational perspective on giving. It is impossible to win over your external audiences if your staff and leadership have not adopted and endorsed this approach. Once you have organizational buy-in, the case serves as a constant reminder and educational tool to ensure you stay on this path. Many charities lose their focus when board members change or a new executive director is hired. An internal case, with buy-in from the existing executive director and board, will ensure that the culture shift you create will last.

The philanthropic planning case has ten core elements, including:

◆ Description of the long-term mission and historical significance of your organization

◆ Definitions of legacy and endowment gifts

◆ Stories of donors who have made significant legacy and endowment gifts in the past that support your organization today, including the impact those gifts have had on those you serve and the long-term outcomes those gifts have created for your organization

◆ How legacy and endowment gifts will help your donors create their own legacies with your organization to ensure your long-term future

◆ How legacy and endowment gifts will fit with your donors' overall plans for the present and future generations of their families, to ensure a meaningful legacy beyond your organization

◆ Organization's values and philosophy about long-term resource management, including legacy and endowment policies

◆ Information about specific tools that help donors achieve long-term objectives for the charity, for themselves, and their families

◆ Information about donor recognition and stewardship to ensure that the charity maintains the legacy for all time

◆ The name and position of the person at your organization who coordinates efforts to encourage legacy and endowment gifts

◆ A clear commitment to donor-focused service and confidentiality

The goal articulated by the philanthropic planning case is not a dollar goal. Instead, it is a goal of sustainability using this approach, even during difficult times. The true measure of success for the case is how effectively the organization engages donors in the long-term mission and their desire to support your organization not for just today, but in perpetuity.

The focus of the philanthropic planning case is to encourage a culture at your organization that supports and encourages donor-focused relationships that lead to legacy and endowment gifts. The relationships are not between individual donors and fundraisers, but relationships among individual donors, their families, their advisors, and your organization. Donors tied to your mission become long-term supporters. By engaging their families in the process, you ensure that their legacies will be carried out, and you may even find a new generation of potential donors.

A true donor-focused gift planning approach also invites all of the advisors working with your donors to participate in the process. A strong case will focus on why these kinds of gifts are important to your organization. It ensures that you maintain a gift planning culture and your program is supported by proper resources now and in the future.

The philanthropic planning case statement has six main uses:

◆ *Change the culture*—The case statement reminds your volunteer board and staff how a donor-focused gift planning approach enhances your charity's mission today and tomorrow.

◆ *Tell the story*—Volunteers and staff need to be reminded of the impact and outcomes of gifts. The stories of matured legacy and endowment gifts are rich fodder to show impact and outcomes. Not just the immediate impact a gift has when it matures, but the impact it has later. For example, not when that building is built, but when it is used to care for sick animals that are adopted by loving families. The reach of these gifts is long term—if you tell some of the really long-term stories, it demonstrates the power of these gifts to fulfill your mission.

◆ *Obtain feedback*—Volunteers and staff often have reasons not to support legacy and endowment gifts. Sharing the case allows you to hear those thoughts and build consensus on the importance of long-term support.

◆ *Form the basis for communications materials*—The stories outlined in the case statement can be reworked to show donors and prospects the long-term outcomes created by future gifts.

◆ *Test the market*—The case statement allows you to determine if your organization is ready to pursue future and endowment gifts. If you face significant opposition to adopting a well-articulated case, you need to spend more time educating volunteers and staff about the importance of these approaches, as your organization is not yet ready for donor-focused gift planning. However, feedback will help you to refine your message so that it "hits the target." When your case is not compelling, it will fail with insiders and potential donors alike.

◆ *Recruit volunteer leadership*—The case statement shares your philosophy with prospective volunteer leaders. If they do not agree with the case, it gives you an opportunity to educate them or to avoid putting them on your board.

To assist you in the creation of your own case statement, review the template case that follows beginning on the next page.

Internal Case for Gift Planning

[YOUR CHARITY]

Statement of Purpose, Mission, and History

[INSERT STATEMENT ABOUT THE MISSION OF YOUR CHARITY, ITS PURPOSE, AND HISTORY; INCLUDE INFORMATION ABOUT ANY PLANNED GIFTS THAT MAY HAVE BEEN MADE IN THE FOUNDING OF YOUR ORGANIZATION]

What is Donor-focused Gift Planning?

Gift planning is a powerful and meaningful way for individuals to give to [YOUR CHARITY] to ensure our long-term future while also meeting personal planning objectives.

Planned gifts (also called legacy gifts, future gifts or deferred gifts) are constructed in the present by donors, but usually do not benefit [YOUR CHARITY] until some future date. Planned gifts generally take two forms, revocable and irrevocable. Revocable planned gifts allow donors to make commitments now but reserve the right to alter their plans up until death. The most common types of revocable planned gifts include naming [YOUR CHARITY] as the beneficiary of a will, living trust, life insurance policy, payable/transfer-on-death account, or retirement account. Irrevocable planned gifts are binding commitments now that provide for [YOUR CHARITY] in the future. Most often, they take the form of life-income gifts including charitable gift annuities, pooled income funds, and charitable remainder trusts.

Donor-focused philanthropy is an emerging model for raising funds. Instead of asking what donors can do for [YOUR CHARITY], it asks what donors need to accomplish for themselves, their families, and their future using a values-based approach. It seeks what is really important to them in their lives. It then asks how [YOUR CHARITY] and other charities they support can be integrated into their tax, estate, and financial planning to help meet these goals. The tools of donor-focused gift planning combine the best of planned giving and donor-focused philanthropy to provide donors with the ability to meet both their personal planning objectives and their philanthropic goals to leave a more meaningful and lasting legacy.

The Important Roles of Endowments at [YOUR CHARITY]

To maximize impact and long-term outcomes, the majority of planned gifts are designated for endowments. Endowments funds are invested to provide future cash flow for [YOUR CHARITY]. Some endowments provide the net income earned by the fund each year, while others use a trustee-determined draw rate. [DESCRIBE ONE OR TWO EXISTING ENDOWMENT GIFTS THAT HAVE ALREADY BEEN RECEIVED AND PROVIDE SUPPORT FOR EXISTING PROGRAMS.] These gifts illustrate one of two important ways that [YOUR CHARITY] uses endowments, to ensure the long-term future and viability of [YOUR CHARITY]. There are no more-important gifts, as without these gifts [YOUR CHARITY] would have to rely solely on operating funds and current gifts, both of which can drop dramatically when the economy is uncertain.

[DESCRIBE ONE OR TWO EXISTING ENDOWMENT GIFTS THAT HAVE ALREADY BEEN RECEIVED AND WERE USED TO FUND NEW PROGRAMS] This type of gift illustrates the second use of endowments, to fund and pursue new programs that it could not otherwise offer due to limited financial resources. Without the [ENDOWMENT NAME] Endowment, [DESCRIBE A SPECIFIC OUTCOME/RESULT THAT WOULD NOT HAVE HAPPENED WITHOUT THE CREATION OF THE ENDOWMENT]

Properly designed, constructed, managed, and stewarded endowments strengthen the long-term well-being of [YOUR CHARITY] by assuring a base of support. More importantly, they provide the means for our donors to impact our future.

Why Should [YOUR CHARITY] Pursue Gift Planning Now?

The United States is currently experiencing the largest intergenerational transfer of wealth in our history. Each year, approximately $23 billion is passed to charitable organizations through wills. In 2013, two of the ten largest gifts to charity were bequests. These gifts, totaling $962 million, made up nearly 25 percent of the total gifts from the top ten individual donors for the year. Because this wealth is transferred when the donor no longer needs it to live on, bequest gifts are the largest gifts that donors can and do make.

Gifts that Continue, Even in a Down Economy

Planned gifts continue to be created and mature regardless of the economy. During difficult economic times, people are more likely to update their wills. Concerns about current income, the value of investments, and decreasing retirement savings cause individuals to postpone philanthropy or consider planned gifts, since they do not impact the donor until death. Legacy Leaders recently completed an analysis of giving patterns since 1966, using data from Giving USA. They found that while giving from individuals, foundations, and corporations either remained static or declined during recession years, planned gifts actually grew by 5 percent during recession years. This allows future gift revenue to serve as a "lifeboat" for [YOUR CHARITY] when all other forms of revenue, including endowment spending amounts, are going down.

Broad Appeal—Everyone Is a Gift Planning Prospect

Recent studies have debunked several myths about gift planning prospects. The 2007 study, Bequest Donors: Demographics and Motivations of Potential and Actual Donors" (Bequest Study), conducted by the Center on Philanthropy at Indiana University (CPIU), found that the majority of individuals still do not have a will. Of those who do, only 7.5 percent have included a charitable provision. When asked why, the number one response in the 2000 National Committee on Planned Giving (now Partnership for Philanthropic Planning) study of donor behavior indicated that donors did not include a charitable bequest because it had never occurred to them. The Bequest Study also showed that donors age forty to sixty are significantly more likely to consider a charitable bequest than donors over age sixty, and that wealth level is not a factor in whether a donor considers a charitable bequest. Individuals engaged in [YOUR CHARITY]'s mission and focused on what it can accomplish are the best future gift prospects, regardless of age or wealth.

Increased Overall Support

The Bequest Study showed that donors who had included a charitable bequest in their plans made annual gifts more than double in size than their counterparts who had not included charity in their estate plans. There are many reasons for this, including that the donor has elevated the charity to the status of a family member and has a much greater investment in the charity's success, and that the donor is providing greater lifetime support to a program that will be endowed later by a bequest. Gift planning will increase not only long-term support but also current support from [YOUR CHARITY]'s most loyal and engaged donors.

We Are Ready

[INSERT LANGUAGE ABOUT YOUR CHARITY'S MOST RECENT STRATEGIC PLANNING PROCESS AND THE NEED FOR RESOURCES FOR LONG-TERM SUPPORT] To implement the plan, [YOUR CHARITY] will need to increase current revenue as well as endowment. With clearly articulated immediate and long-term goals, we are prepared to share with prospects the impact they can have today and the outcomes they can create for tomorrow. We have a robust group of regular, consistent donors, the type of people who are the most likely to consider and create planned gifts. [YOUR CHARITY] is committed to a long-term approach, with endowment and gift policies that ensure confidentiality and that donor wishes will be fulfilled. We have developed a stewardship program to share successes with donors and their families, illustrating the immediate impact and long-term outcomes created by their gifts. [INDICATE THAT RESOURCES HAVE BEEN DESIGNATED TO FUND THIS PROJECT FOR THE LONG TERM AND NAME THE POINT PERSON DESIGNATED TO IMPLEMENT THE PROGRAM]

Most importantly, we have a compelling mission, [RESTATE MISSION AND OUTCOMES CREATED BY PAST ENDOWMENTS OR PLANNED GIFTS]. Our gift planning program, if properly built and maintained, will allow us to pursue the next generation of endowments and long-term support to ensure our future.

Gift Counting and Recognition

Gift counting and recognition are hot button issues for charities. Too often, charities ignore this important area until faced with a donor who wants far more recognition than the gift deserves. Without a *formal* policy, the organization has no leg to stand on and usually grants the donor's request, even though it is not in the best interest of the organization. Worse still, other donors see that example and then ask for similar treatment, leading to bad counting, bad naming, and charities overstating their fundraising results.

To combat bad naming and recognition policies, the Council for Advancement and Support of Education (CASE), the Partnership for Philanthropic Planning (PPP), and the Association for Healthcare Philanthropy (AHP) each created gift counting standards. These national organizations worked long and hard to put together their policies, but could not agree in every detail about how counting and recognition should work. As you build your gift planning program, we recommend that you adopt the PPP standards as they pay special attention to planned gifts. To download the PPP standards, visit *pppnet.org*.

The PPP standards suggest a system that has your organization count three separate numbers that should not be added together. They are:

1. ***Category A—Outright Gifts:*** The total of outright gifts and pledges received, reported at face value.

2. ***Category B—Irrevocable Deferred Gifts:*** The total of irrevocable deferred commitments, which will be received at an undetermined time in the future, reported at face value.

3. ***Category C—Revocable Gifts:*** The total of revocable deferred commitments, which may be received at an undetermined time in the future, reported at estimated current value.

Using this methodology, your organization has complete transparency for your donors.

Gift Counting and Recognition Policy Summary

_____ (hereinafter "[YOUR CHARITY]") has adopted the Council for Advancement and Support of Education gift counting standards for counting outright gifts and the Partnership for Philanthropic Planning (PPP) gift counting standards for counting planned gifts. For complete details, please refer to the [YOUR CHARITY] Gift Acceptance Policy, *http://pppnet.org/guidelinesforreporting*, and the CASE Reporting Standards and Management Guidelines, 4th Edition.

Gift counting and reporting apply to all gifts generally and for fundraising campaigns. Recognition or crediting does not stem from any of the factors of counting and reporting, although [YOUR CHARITY] generally uses its gift counting amount as the basis for gift recognition. In some cases, however, [YOUR CHARITY] will recognize a gift for an amount other than the counting amount. For example, if John and Susan Jones, husband and wife, each give [YOUR CHARITY] $500,000, we may recognize them both as $1 million donors because their joint giving totals this amount. Similarly, [YOUR CHARITY] gives a donor "soft-credit" for recognition purposes when a corporate matching gift is received as a result of the donor making his or her own contribution. Because gift recognition is fundamentally different than gift counting and reporting, it is covered in Section IX of [YOUR CHARITY]'s Gift Acceptance Policy.

Gift Counting and Reporting

The CASE Reporting Standards suggest that charities report two numbers for their fundraising results. The first number is the total of outright gifts and pledges received, reported at face value. The second number is the total of irrevocable deferred commitments, reported at face and present value, using the IRS income tax charitable deduction as a proxy for a true present value calculation. Revocable deferred commitments are not reported.

[YOUR CHARITY] recognizes that these standards substantially under-report the value of both irrevocable and revocable deferred commitments, thereby making them less attractive to prospective donors, even though they are potentially the largest gifts many prospects can make. These standards also make it difficult when reviewing a gift report, particularly during a campaign, to determine which funds are available now, which funds will not be accessible until the future, and which funds may not be received at all. Finally, such standards create an incentive for gift officers to solicit outright gifts when a future gift may better serve both the donor and [YOUR CHARITY]. With this in mind, [YOUR CHARITY] has adopted the PPP gift counting standards for both irrevocable and revocable deferred commitments, or what [YOUR CHARITY] calls future gifts.

Under its gift acceptance policy, [YOUR CHARITY] adheres to the following gift reporting standards:

Three Separate Reporting Numbers

1. Category A—Outright Gifts: The total of outright gifts and pledges received, reported at face value.

2. Category B—Irrevocable Deferred Gifts: The total of irrevocable deferred commitments, which will be received at an undetermined time in the future, reported at face value.

3. Category C—Revocable Gifts: The total of revocable deferred commitments, which may be received at an undetermined time in the future, reported at estimated current value.

When to Report Gifts: Outright gifts are reported only when assets are transferred irrevocably to [YOUR CHARITY] or a gift intention is executed. Deferred irrevocable gifts should be reported only when assets are transferred to the gift instrument. Revocable commitments should be reported when the gift instrument is executed and sufficient documentation is received by [YOUR CHARITY].

What to Report: All gifts, pledges, and commitments falling into categories covered by these standards may be reported. However, in keeping with the spirit of these standards, it is never appropriate to add all three categories together and report only one number when announcing gift results.

Category A: Outright Gifts

1. Definition: Gifts that are usable or will become usable for institutional purposes including:

    a. Cash

    b. Marketable securities

    c. Other current gifts of noncash assets

    d. Irrevocable pledges collectible during the reporting period (five years or the campaign period, whichever is greater)

    e. The gift portion of bargain sales

    f. Lead trust distributions received during the reporting period (five years or the campaign period, whichever is greater)

    g. Cash value of life insurance owned by [YOUR CHARITY] (net of policy loans)

    h. Realized life insurance or retirement plan benefits in excess of the amounts previously counted

    i. Realized bequests in excess of the amounts previously counted

2. Statement of Intent: Statements of Intent are counted upon receipt of the written intention, provided the intention is in accord with these guidelines.

    a. Intentions to Make Outright Gifts: Such intentions should be written and should commit to a specific dollar amount that will be paid according to a fixed time schedule. The payment period, regardless of when the intention is made, should not exceed five years. Therefore, an intention received even on the last day of a campaign is counted in campaign totals and may be paid over a five-year period.

    b. Oral Statements of Intent: Oral intentions should not be reported in giving or campaign totals. On the rare occasion when an exception is warranted, [YOUR CHARITY] should write to the individual making an oral pledge to document the commitment, place a copy of the confirmation in the donor's file, and gain specific, written approval from the Gift Acceptance Committee.

3. Guidelines for Reporting Specific Types of Assets

   a. Cash: Report cash at full value as of the date received by [YOUR CHARITY].

   b. Marketable Securities: Marketable securities should be counted according to the IRS standards then in effect for gifts of this type. The current standard values a gift of marketable securities at the average of the high and low quoted selling prices on the gift date (the date the donor relinquished dominion and control of the assets in favor of [YOUR CHARITY]). If there were not any actual trades on the gift date, the fair market value can be computed using the weighted average of the mean of the high and low trading prices on a date before and a date after the gift date, if those dates are a reasonable number of days before and after the actual gift date. If there were no actual trades in a reasonable number of days before and after the gift date, then the fair market value is computed based on the average of the bid and the ask price on the gift date. Exactly when dominion and control has been relinquished by a donor depends on the method of delivery of the securities to [YOUR CHARITY]. These reporting standards do not address the multitude of tax rules regarding the delivery of securities by the donor to [YOUR CHARITY].

   c. Closely-Held Stock:

      i. Gifts of closely-held stock exceeding $10,000 in value should be reported at the fair market value placed on them by a qualified independent appraiser as required by the IRS for valuing gifts of nonpublicly traded stock. Gifts of $10,000 or less may be valued at the per-share cash purchase price of the closest transaction. Normally, this transaction will be the redemption of the stock by the corporation.

      ii. If no redemption is consummated during the reporting period, a gift of closely-held stock may be credited to gift or campaign totals at the value determined by a qualified independent appraiser. For a gift of $10,000 or less, when no redemption has occurred during the reporting period, an independent CPA who maintains the books for a closely-held corporation is deemed to be qualified to value the stock of the corporation.

   d. Gifts of Property:

      i. Gifts of real and personal property that qualify for a charitable deduction should be counted at their full fair market value. Gifts-in-kind, such as equipment and software, shall be counted at their fair market value.

      ii. Caution should be exercised to ensure that only gifts that are convertible to cash or that are of actual direct value to [YOUR CHARITY] are counted. Megagifts of software and hardware may require special care. These types of gifts can be especially complex, and [YOUR CHARITY] should exercise extreme caution in counting these gifts in gift totals. Gifts with fair market value exceeding $5,000 should be counted at the value placed on them by a qualified independent appraiser as required by the IRS for valuing noncash charitable contributions. Gifts of $5,000 and under may be reported at the value declared by the donor or placed on them by a qualified expert.

    e. Nongovernmental Grants and Contracts: Grant income from private, nongovernmental sources should be reported; contract revenue should be excluded. The difference between a private grant and contract should be judged on the basis of the intention of the awarding agency and the legal obligation incurred by [YOUR CHARITY] in accepting the award. A grant is bestowed voluntarily without expectation of any tangible compensation. It is donative in nature. A contract carries an explicit quid pro quo relationship between the source and [YOUR CHARITY].

    f. Realized Testamentary Gifts: All realized bequests should be counted at full value in gift totals, insofar as the amount received exceeds commitments counted previously. If a revocable testamentary commitment made during a current counting period and counted in Category C matures during the same counting period, it should be removed from Category C and included as an outright gift in Category A.

    g. Realized Retirement Plan Assets: All realized gifts of retirement plan assets should be counted at full face value in gift totals to the extent the gift was not counted previously.

4. Gifts in Contemplation of a Campaign: From time to time, [YOUR CHARITY] will engage in comprehensive and targeted fundraising campaigns. It is often the case that certain prospects, to meet their own personal planning objectives or to help [YOUR CHARITY] launch the initiative, will make gifts before the official "start date" of the campaign, in contemplation of the fundraising effort. In such cases, the Gift Acceptance Committee shall make a recommendation of all gifts that should be counted and reported in the campaign, even though such gifts were received before the official start date of the campaign.

Category B: Irrevocable Deferred

1. Definition: Gifts committed during the reporting period, but likely usable by the organization only at some point after the end of the period, including:

    a. Split-Interest Gifts, such as charitable gift annuities, pooled income funds, and charitable remainder trusts, in which the beneficiary designation is irrevocable

    b. Gifts of a Remainder Interest in a Personal Residence or Farm with a Retained Life Estate

    c. Death Benefit of Paid-up Life Insurance in which the charity is both owner and beneficiary

    d. Irrevocable Testamentary Pledges or Contract to Make a Will

    e. Lead Trust Distributions to be made after the reporting period

2. Charitable Remainder Trusts, Pooled Income Funds and Gift Annuities: Gifts made to establish charitable remainder trusts for which the remainder is not subject to change or revocation, pooled income fund gifts, and gifts to fund charitable gift annuities should be counted at face value. When additions are made to gifts that have been counted previously, the additions can be counted at face value. Counting deferred gifts at face value meets

several critical needs. First, in a donor-focused environment, the donor is getting gift credit for the amount of assets actually transferred to fund a life-income gift. While these assets may be worth less to the charity due to the income interest retained by the donor, the donor likely feels like the gift was the face value amount. Second, by counting such gifts at face value, it creates an incentive for the fundraisers to use a donor-focused approach in their donor work. If the fundraiser were to only receive credit for the net present value of a gift, the fundraiser might push a donor to an alternative gift option that gave the fundraiser more credit but did not meet the needs of the donor. By counting at face value, the interests of the donor remain paramount.

3. Charitable/Deferred Pledge Agreement: A deferred pledge agreement is a legally binding document that places an obligation on the estate of the issuer to transfer a certain amount to [YOUR CHARITY]. Under such an agreement, the executor of the donor's estate is held legally responsible for payment of the specified amount from the estate.

4. Remainder Interest in a Personal Residence or Farm with Retained Life Estate: A gift of a remainder interest in a personal residence or farm should be counted at the face value of the remainder interest.

5. Charitable Lead Trusts: Charitable lead trusts are gifts in trust that pay an income to the charity over a period of time. These payments should be counted in Category A for amounts received during the campaign period (or during the next five-year period if not in a campaign). The remainder of the payments to be received by [YOUR CHARITY] should be counted in Category B.

Category C: Revocable Deferred Gifts

1. Definition: Gifts solicited and committed during the reporting period, but for which the donor retains the right to change the commitment and/or beneficiary, including:

    a. Estate Provisions, either from a will or a living trust.

    b. Charitable Remainder Trusts in which the donor retains the right to change the beneficiary designation. When additions are made to gifts that have been counted previously, the additions can be counted in the current reporting period.

    c. IRAs or Other Retirement Plan Assets in which [YOUR CHARITY]'s interest remains revocable by the donor.

    d. Life Insurance in which the Donor Retains Ownership (face value less any policy loans) and in which [YOUR CHARITY] is owner but premiums remain due.

    e. Other Revocable Pledges

2. Uncertainty of Revocable Commitments: It is difficult to put specific numbers on certain revocable commitments when the ultimate maturation value is uncertain, or if it is uncertain that the gift will mature to [YOUR CHARITY] at all. Examples include [YOUR CHARITY] being named the beneficiary of a trust to which another person retains access to principal, or a contingent bequest that relies upon another person predeceasing the donor for any funds

to come to [YOUR CHARITY]. The numbers reported in Category C should be best estimates and reflect both a conservative and realistic understanding of each donor's circumstances. If the commitment is difficult to value or will likely be nominal, it should be counted in Category C at $1. If the gift matures at a date in the future, the full value can then be counted in Category A.

3. Estate Provisions: To include estate provisions in giving totals, the following requirements must be satisfied:

   a. The commitment should specify an amount to be distributed to [YOUR CHARITY] or, if a percentage of the estate or a trust, specify a credible estimate of the value of the estate at the time the commitment is made. If a credible estimate is not possible, then [YOUR CHARITY] shall use a rolling five-year average of all bequests received. Until a five-year average can be calculated, an estimated value of $50,000 shall be used. (Note that for the top one hundred planned giving programs in the United States, the average bequest is approximately $240,000, according to a study by Changing Our World completed in 2008.)

   b. Have verification of the commitment through one of the following forms:

      i. A letter or agreement from the donor or donor's advisor affirming the commitment

      ii. Copy of will

      iii. Notification form provided by [YOUR CHARITY], signed by donor or advisor

   c. [YOUR CHARITY] will carefully investigate the actual circumstances underlying the estate and be conservative in counting such commitments toward gift totals. If any circumstances should make it unlikely that the amount pledged by bequest will actually be realized by [YOUR CHARITY], then the commitment should be further adjusted according to specific circumstances, or reported at $1.

4. Retirement Plan Assets:

   a. [YOUR CHARITY] may be named as the beneficiary of retirement plan assets. A testamentary pledge of retirement plan assets shall be included in gift totals if the following requirements have been satisfied:

   b. There must be a means to establish a credible estimate of the value of the retirement plan account at the time the commitment is made. If a credible estimate is not possible, then [YOUR CHARITY] shall use a rolling five-year average of all bequests received. Until a five-year average can be calculated, an estimated value of $50,000 shall be used.

      i. Have verification of the commitment in the form of a letter from the donor or the donor's advisor affirming the commitment.

      ii. [YOUR CHARITY] will carefully investigate the actual circumstances underlying the plan and be conservative in counting such commitments toward gift totals. If any circumstances should make it unlikely that the amount pledged will actually be realized by [YOUR CHARITY], then the commitment should be further adjusted according to specific circumstances, or reported at $1.

Gifts That May Be Counted in More than One Category, Depending on the Circumstances

1. Life Insurance: To include commitments of life insurance in gift totals, these requirements must be satisfied:

   a. Ownership:

      i. [YOUR CHARITY] should be made the owner and irrevocable beneficiary of gifts of all new policies, paid-up policies, and existing policies that are not fully paid up.

      ii. If [YOUR CHARITY] is the beneficiary only and not the owner of a policy, gift credit will be given but only in Category C, in the same way as credit is given to any other revocable gift commitment.

      iii. The remainder of these guidelines assumes that [YOUR CHARITY] is the owner of the policy.

   b. Paid-up Life Insurance Policies: Counted at face value in Category B.

   c. Existing Policies/Not Fully Paid Up: A life insurance policy that is not fully paid up on the date of contribution should be counted at face value only in Category C.

   d. New Policies: Face amount of these policies should be counted in Category C.

   e. Realized Death Benefits: The insurance company's settlement amount for an insurance policy whose death benefit is realized during the campaign period, whether the policy is owned by [YOUR CHARITY] or not, should be counted in gift totals, less amounts previously counted in former campaigns.

2. Wholly Charitable Trusts Administered by Others:

   a. A wholly charitable trust is one that is held for the irrevocable benefit of [YOUR CHARITY], where the principal is invested and the income is distributed to us. All interests in income and principal are irrevocably dedicated to charitable purposes (as opposed to a charitable remainder or lead trust). While it is similar in that sense to an endowment fund, it is created as a freestanding entity.

   b. The fair market value of the assets, or a portion of the assets, of such a trust administered by an outside fiduciary, should be counted in Category A, in the "gifts and pledges" section of gift totals, for the year in which the trust is established, provided that [YOUR CHARITY] has an irrevocable right to all or a predetermined portion of the income of the trust. If the trustee retains or is awarded the right to designate or alter the income beneficiary, only the income should be reported and then only as it distributed.

c. In cases where less than the entire income of the trust is to be distributed to [YOUR CHARITY], the amount to be reported is the income to be distributed to [YOUR CHARITY] over the total income (or the stated percentage to be distributed, if the trust terms spell this out as a percentage) multiplied by the value of the trust assets. The income of the trust, thereafter, is reported as a gift.

d. Community and Private Foundations: Gifts to community foundations, the income from which is irrevocably designated, in whole or in part, to [YOUR CHARITY], and private foundations established solely to benefit [YOUR CHARITY] or where [YOUR CHARITY] is to receive a specified percentage of the annual income each year, are two examples of wholly charitable trusts administered by others. (Gift credit will generally be given to the foundation, although the original donors or their families should certainly be kept apprised of the distributions if at all possible and given recognition credit.)

e. Donor-Advised Funds: Donor-advised funds are IRS-approved public charities generally managed by investment companies and community foundations that serve as conduits for gifts. The donor's contribution is made to the fund. The donor reserves the right to suggest which charities should receive the annual income. Gifts from DAFs will be counted like any other gift as received. If [YOUR CHARITY] is entitled to receive a certain percentage of the annual distributions of a DAF, it may count the value of that percentage as if it were an irrevocable trust administered by others.

Gifts That Change Character During a Counting or Campaign

1. All campaigns face the dilemma of reporting commitments that change character during the campaign period. A commitment should, at the end of the campaign period, be reported only once and should reflect the final (or most recent) form of the commitment.

2. It is possible for a donor to establish an irrevocable deferred gift or a revocable gift commitment that would be reported in Categories B or C, and then, for that gift to mature within the same campaign. In such cases, the cumulative campaign report will recognize the gift only in Category A, and any previous interim report of the gift in Categories B or C is deleted. The annual report would note this change as well.

    a. Example: A donor creates a charitable remainder trust, but retains the right to change the remainder beneficiary. That commitment would appear in Category C. If, later in the campaign period, the donor made the remainder beneficiary irrevocable, the commitment would shift in the cumulative campaign report to Category B and be removed from Category C. The annual report would note the shift as well.

    b. Example: [YOUR CHARITY] is named as the payment beneficiary of a 20-year charitable lead trust paying $10,000 per year ($200,000 in total) in the first year of a seven-year comprehensive campaign. The annual report in year one will note $10,000 (the amount actually received that year) in Category A and $190,000 in Category B. The cumulative comprehensive campaign report (covering all seven years) will report $70,000 in Category A (the amount committed and to be received during the campaign period) and $130,000 in Category B. In years two through seven, the annual report will again count a $10,000 cash gift with a note that this commitment had previously been reported in Category B. There would be no further reporting in the annual report for the Category B portion of the gift since there had been no new commitment in year two.

All gifts are "counted" at face value, regardless of the type of gift, the date of maturity, or even the likelihood of maturity. However, everyone knows that Category A gifts are current gifts for certain now, Category B gifts are future gifts for certain at an unknown time, and Category C gifts are future gifts that may or may not mature to your organization.

No longer will your charity have to worry about showing someone who has named you as the beneficiary on a $1 million face term life insurance policy as a $1 million donor. Instead, that donor is placed in Category C, so your charity is not depending on a gift that is not likely to ever mature to your benefit.

When it comes time to recognize these donors, most organization recognize donors in Categories A and B at face value and while they may list donors from Category C, they do not offer naming or other perks since these gifts are revocable.

Gift Acceptance Policies

Most charities developed gift acceptance policies in anticipation of their last campaign and have not reviewed them since. Or worse still, they simply have no gift acceptance policies whatsoever. Then, a donor appears with a parcel of real estate allegedly worth $10 million and the organization jumps through hoops to accept it, only discovering later that it was previously an apple orchard and contaminated with arsenic which will require $12 million to clean up.

If this does not sound familiar, don't worry, it will happen to your organization eventually. The problem with the real estate might be different. For example, it could be landlocked with no access, a former gas station, or underwater—literally or subject to more debt than it's worth. The list goes on. Unfortunately, as long as there are unscrupulous people, your charity will be offered seemingly valuable gifts that actually will cost you more to dispose of than they are worth.

The worst time to be evaluating your gift acceptance policy is when you are confronted with a big gift that your organization could really use. By drafting a gift acceptance policy now, you will know exactly:

◆ What you can take

◆ What you cannot take

◆ What steps you need to take to evaluate gifts when they are offered

With a good policy in place, you are much less likely to accept a bad asset or a gift structured in such a way that it hurts, rather than helps, your organization long term.

GIFT ACCEPTANCE POLICY

[YOUR CHARITY]

[YOUR CHARITY] (the "Charity"), a nonprofit organization incorporated in the State of _____, encourages the solicitation and acceptance of gifts to further and fulfill its mission of (insert your mission statement here).

I. Purpose of Policies

This statement articulates the policies of the Board of Directors (the "Board") of the Charity concerning the acceptance of charitable gifts and guides prospective donors and their advisors when making gifts to the Charity. The Advancement Committee of the Board will adopt appropriate procedures to implement these policies.

II. Responsibility to Donors

A. Commitment to a Donor-Focused, Philanthropic Approach: The Charity, its staff, and volunteer representatives shall endeavor to assist donors in accomplishing their philanthropic objectives in a donor-focused way. In many circumstances, this may involve the donor's professional advisors, as charitable support is often integrated with a donor's overall tax, estate, and financial planning.

B. Confidentiality: Information concerning all transactions between a donor and the Charity shall be held by the Charity in confidence, and may be disclosed only with the permission of the donor or the donor's designee.

C. Anonymity: The Charity shall respect the wishes of any donor offering anonymous support and will implement reasonable procedures to safeguard such donor's identity.

D. Ethical Standards: The charity is committed to the highest ethical standards. The Charity, its staff, and volunteer representatives shall adhere to both the Model Standards of Practice for the Charitable Gift Planner, as adopted by the Partnership for Philanthropic Planning ("PPP"), and the Code of Ethical Principles and Standards as adopted by the Association of Fundraising Professionals ("AFP"). The Charity will not participate in gift discussions if there is a question as to the title/ownership of the asset or the donor's competency to transfer an asset.

III. Legal Considerations

A. Compliance: The Charity shall comply with all local, state, and federal laws and regulations concerning all charitable gifts it encourages, solicits, or accepts. All required disclosures, registrations, and procedures shall be made and/or followed in a thorough and timely manner.

B. Endorsement of Providers: The Charity shall not endorse legal, tax, or financial advisors to prospective donors.

C. Finder's Fees and Commissions: The Charity shall not pay fees to any person as consideration for directing a gift by a donor to the Charity.

D. Legal, Tax and Financial Advice: The Charity shall inform prospective donors that it does not provide legal, tax or financial advice, and shall encourage prospective donors to discuss all charitable gift planning decisions with their own advisors before entering into any commitments to make gifts to the Charity.

E. Preparation of Legal Documents: The Charity shall not prepare legal documents for execution by donors, except forms to create charitable gift annuities. The Charity may provide model language, such as sample bequest language, gift agreements, or charitable remainder trusts, but shall strongly encourage prospective donors to have this language reviewed by their own counsel.

F. Payment of Fees: It will be the responsibility of the donor to secure an appraisal (where required) and to pay for the advice of independent legal, financial, or other professional advisors as needed for all gifts made to the Charity.

G. Service as Executor or Living Trust Trustee: Unless approved in advance by the Vice President of Finance, the Charity will not agree to serve as executor of a decedent's estate or as trustee of a living trust or other trust intended to serve as a person's primary estate planning document.

H. Trusteeship: The Charity may serve as trustee of trusts to maintain its gift annuity reserve accounts, as required by relevant state insurance law, in connection with the Charity's gift annuity program. The Charity may serve as trustee of charitable remainder trusts, provided that 100 percent of the remainder interest in the trust is irrevocably dedicated to the Charity, and the charitable remainder trust meets the minimum standards set forth in the Gift Acceptance Procedures. The Charity may serve as a trustee of trusts only in circumstances in which its investment authority as trustee is unrestricted. The Charity will not serve as cotrustee of a charitable trust.

I. Use of Counsel: The Charity shall seek the advice of legal counsel in matters relating to the acceptance of gifts when appropriate. Review by counsel is recommended for gifts involving: closely-held stock transfers that are subject to restrictions; gifts involving contracts, such as bargain sales; reformation of charitable trusts; and transactions involving potential conflicts of interest.

IV. Gift Acceptance

A. Implementation: Gift acceptance, as outlined in these policies, is delegated by the Board to the Vice President of Advancement (the "Vice President"). The Vice President is authorized to accept all gifts permitted by this policy.

B. Approval of Exceptions: Acceptance of gifts outside the scope of this policy requires the unanimous, written approval of the Gift Acceptance Committee (the "GAC"). The Vice President shall report all gifts accepted as exceptions to the policy to the Advancement Committee of the Board at its next regular meeting.

C. Gift Acceptance Committee: The GAC shall be made up of the Chair of the Advancement Committee of the Board, the Vice President, and the Vice President of Finance.

D. Gift Acceptance Procedures: The Board delegates to the GAC the responsibility of approving Gift Acceptance Procedures to implement these policies.

E. Gift Acceptance Alternatives: In the event the GAC rejects a gift, the Charity will attempt to assist the donor in finding a suitable third-party charity to accept the gift and share the proceeds, less costs, with the Charity.

F. Gift Agreements: The Charity generally uses nonbinding statements of intent to document gift commitments. The GAC shall create and maintain samples for use by staff and volunteer leadership. All statements of intent shall include a short profile of the donor, the donor's commitment and timeframe for payments, the Charity's commitment (including restrictions), how the completed gift will be managed, alternative use and saving language, stewardship, and donor recognition.

> ### It's Better to Replace than to Adjust
>
> Many organizations already have a gift acceptance policy in place. It has been our experience that it is easier to simply replace the existing policy than to try and take elements from this template policy and insert them into the existing policy. You need to make your own decision on how to handle this issue, but we strongly encourage you to consider replacing your existing policy rather than trying to adjust it.
>
> **observation**

1. Unrestricted Commitments Within a Fiscal Year: The Charity does not require statements of intent for unrestricted gift commitments within the current fiscal year.

2. Unrestricted Commitments Covering More Than One Fiscal Year: If the unrestricted commitment covers more than one fiscal year, a simple letter or card documenting the gift amount and payment schedule may be substituted for a formal statement of intent.

3. Commitments Subject to Restrictions: The Charity requires an executed statement of intent for all commitments subject to restrictions, including restricted endowment gifts.

4. Commitments Over $1 million: The Charity requires an executed, binding gift agreement (pledge) for all commitments over $1 million unless waived in writing by the Vice President.

V. Gift Restrictions

A. Unrestricted Gifts: To provide the Charity with maximum flexibility in the pursuit of its mission, donors shall always be encouraged to consider unrestricted gifts or gifts restricted to budgeted priorities of the Charity.

B. Budgeted Programs or Facilities: The Charity may accept gifts restricted to specific budgeted programs and purposes.

C. Other Restrictions on Gifts: The Charity may accept gifts restricted to nonbudgeted programs and purposes only upon the prior, written approval of the Vice President. The

Charity reserves the right to decline gifts that are too restrictive in purpose, too difficult to administer, or for purposes outside of its mission.

D. Unrestricted Future Gifts: As donors making large future gifts generally intend for these gifts to benefit the long-term future of the Charity, all future gifts (e.g., bequests, retirement plan, and life insurance designations) with a value over $25,000 shall be added to the Board Designated Unrestricted Endowment.

VI. Types of Property

These assets may be considered for acceptance by the Charity, subject to these criteria:

A. Cash: Acceptable in any negotiable form, including currency, check, and credit card gifts.

B. Securities:

1. Publicly Traded Securities: Stocks, bonds, and mutual funds traded on an exchange or other publicly reported market are acceptable.

2. Closely-Held Securities and Business Interests: Debt and equity positions in nonpublicly traded businesses, hedge funds, REITs, and interests in limited liability companies and partnerships, may only be accepted upon prior written approval of the GAC after review in accordance with the Gift Acceptance Procedures.

3. Options and Other Rights in Securities: Warrants, stock options, and stock appreciation rights may only be accepted upon prior written approval of the GAC.

C. Life Insurance: The Charity will accept a gift of life insurance provided that the policy has a positive cash surrender value and the Charity has been named both beneficiary and irrevocable owner of the policy.

D. Real Property: Personal and commercial real property, real estate interests/derivatives, and remainder interests in property (gifts subject to a retained life estate) may only be accepted upon prior written approval of the GAC after review in accordance with the Gift Acceptance Procedures, including appropriate environmental screenings. The Charity does not accept debt-encumbered real property, real property subject to a mortgage or lien, or time-share interests. For gifts subject to a retained life estate, the donor or primary life beneficiary shall be responsible for all expenses other than capital expenditures during the life tenancy, including but not limited to maintenance, real estate taxes, assessments, and insurance.

E. Tangible Personal Property: Jewelry, books, works of art, collections, equipment, and other property that may be touched, may only be accepted after review in accordance with the Gift Acceptance Procedures.

F. Other Property: Property not otherwise described in this section, whether real or personal, of any description (including but not limited to mortgages, notes, contract rights, copyrights, patents, trademarks, mineral rights, oil and gas interests, and royalties) may be only be accepted upon prior written approval of the GAC.

VII. Structured Current Gifts

    A. Bargain Sales: Transactions wherein the Charity pays less than full value for an asset and issues a gift receipt for the difference may only be accepted upon prior written approval of the GAC after review in accordance with the Gift Acceptance Procedures.

    B. Charitable Lead Trusts: The Charity may accept a designation as payment beneficiary of a charitable lead trust. The Charity will not serve as trustee of a charitable lead trust.

    C. IRA Charitable Rollover: The Charity may accept all gifts directly transferred from an IRA, as permitted under the Pension Protection Act of 2006 and subsequent extensions (if in effect).

    D. Matching Gifts: The Charity will accept all matching gifts, subject to the terms and conditions of Section VI.

    E. Other Structured Current Gifts: The Charity may only accept other structured current gifts with prior written approval of the GAC after review in accordance with the Gift Acceptance Procedures.

VIII. Future Gifts

    A. Future Gifts Subject to a Payment Interest

        1. Charitable Gift Annuities: The Charity offers immediate payment, deferred payment, commuted payment, and flexible payment charitable gift annuities, provided:

            i.   Minimum funding amount: $10,000

            ii.   Maximum funding amount: 25 percent of total gift annuity pool [if pool is unrestricted]; (10 percent of total gift annuity pool if pool is restricted)

            iii.   Minimum age(s): None (All proposals for donors with an average age under sixty shall include an option with a hedge against inflation)

            iv.   Maximum number of lives: Two

            v.   Ultimate beneficiary: The Charity for 100 percent, irrevocably

            vi.   Payout rate: American Council on Gift Annuities recommended rates (All proposals shall include offer of 100 percent, 90 percent, and 80 percent of the ACGA-recommended rate)

            vii.   Payment schedule: Monthly, quarterly, semiannual, or annual

            viii.   Funding assets: Prior written approval of the GAC is required for assets other than cash or publicly traded securities

        2. Charitable Remainder Trusts When the Charity Serves as Trustee: The Charity will serve as trustee of charitable remainder trusts, provided:

    i.   Minimum funding amount: $100,000

    ii.   Maximum funding amount: None

    iii.   Minimum age(s): None

    iv.   Maximum number of lives: None

    v.   Ultimate beneficiary: The Charity for 100 percent, irrevocably

    vi.   Payout rate: Per gift acceptance procedures (generally 5 percent to 7 percent)

    vii. Minimum charitable remainder: 25 percent of the funding amount (using the income tax charitable deduction methodology)

    viii. Payment schedule: Monthly, quarterly, semiannual, or annual

    ix.   Funding assets: Prior written approval of the GAC is required for assets other than cash or publicly traded securities, although a broader array of assets will be approved for a charitable remainder trust than a charitable gift annuity

    x.   Costs charged to the trust: Investment management, administration, legal counsel, and tax return preparation

3. Charitable Remainder Trusts When the Charity Does Not Serve as Trustee: The Charity will accept designation as charitable beneficiary of charitable remainder trusts that do not name the Charity as trustee. Donors who create externally managed and trusteed trusts will be asked to provide the Charity with a copy of the trust document and annual investment reports for record-keeping purposes.

4. Pooled Income Funds: The Charity offers a pooled income fund provided:

    i.   Minimum funding amount: $10,000

    ii.   Maximum funding amount: None

    iii.   Minimum age(s): None

    iv.   Maximum number of lives: Two

    v.   Ultimate beneficiary: The Charity for 100 percent, irrevocably

    vi.   Payout: Net income (capital gains treated as income)

    vii. Payment schedule: Quarterly

    viii. Funding assets: Prior written approval of the GAC is required for assets other than cash or publicly traded securities.

    ix.   Costs charged to the pool: Investment management, administration, legal counsel, and tax return preparation

B. Future Gifts Not Subject to a Payment Interest

1. Gifts by Will or Living Trust: Donors and supporters of the Charity will be encouraged to designate the Charity as a beneficiary of their wills or living trusts.

2. Retirement Plan, Life Insurance, and Other Beneficiary Designations: Donors and supporters of the Charity will be encouraged to designate the Charity as beneficiary or contingent beneficiary of their retirement plans, life insurance policies, and other accounts on which they can name a beneficiary.

IX. Donor Recognition

A. General: The Board, upon the recommendation of the GAC and the Advancement Committee, establish criteria for the recognition, honoring, and stewarding of donors.

B. Buildings: Except in the case of naming opportunities that appear on a schedule approved by the Board, the advancement staff of the Charity shall make no commitments to donors concerning the naming of buildings or facilities without the approval of the Board upon the recommendation of the GAC.

X. Reporting and Valuation Standards

A. Gift Reporting and Counting: For outright gifts, the Charity shall follow the Council for Advancement and Support of Education ("CASE") Reporting Standards and Management Guidelines for Educational Institutions, Fourth Edition, 2009. For future gifts, the Charity shall follow the PPP Guidelines for Reporting and Counting Charitable Gifts, Second Edition, 2009. All exceptions to these standards shall be made by the GAC.

B. Gift Valuation: The Charity shall follow the PPP Valuation Standards for Charitable Planned Gifts. All exceptions to these standards shall be made by the GAC.

XI. Periodic Review

A. Regular Review: The GAC shall review these policies in even-numbered years to ensure they continue to accurately describe the policies of the Charity with respect to acceptance of charitable gifts, and shall propose to the full Board for ratification those revisions the GAC shall determine to be necessary or appropriate.

B. Special Review: The GAC shall initiate a supplemental review of these policies upon the enactment or promulgation of legislation or regulatory rules affecting fundraising and gift acceptance by the Charity, or prior to the start of a formal fundraising campaign. All proposed changes shall be shared with the full Board for ratification.

Start by using the sample. The template includes all of the different sections you should include in your gift acceptance policy. Each section has a clearly defined purpose. If it does not apply to your organization now, consider if it might apply in the future before you eliminate it. Customize the template to create your own gift acceptance policies. You should then review the policy with the development committee of your board and ultimately seek full board approval of the entire policy. Try not to add procedures into your policy; they do not need board approval and will only require repeated trips to the board for revisions.

Gift Agreements

A gift agreement is an understanding between the charity and the donor that outlines the commitments each is making to the other. The agreement can be legally binding or it can simply be a statement of intent that is not binding. A good gift agreement protects the relationship between your organization and a donor by clearly articulating the responsibilities of each party related to the gift.

The need for gift agreements is one of the most-often overlooked components of a fundraising program for new and smaller nonprofits. Gift agreements are not necessarily a gift planning function, but at most nonprofits, they get lumped into gift planning because the person responsible for gift planning is also the most knowledgeable about legal issues facing the charity.

As the Baby Boomers and the generations that follow (i.e., the New Philanthropists born 1946 to the present) become the primary givers in the United States, they will increasingly seek to restrict their gifts. Without an effective gift agreement process and documents, your organization will risk losing future support from these donors, as well as lawsuits if you fail to comply with the terms of those gifts.

A Gift That Spans the Generations

Steve Girard was the richest man in America in 1811. Born of poor parents in France in 1750, he had gone to sea as a teenager and rose through the ranks to become a sea captain and prominent merchant. He became an American in 1778, married an American woman, and lived in Philadelphia.

When the War of 1812 broke out, the US Government rapidly ran out of money, so in 1813, Girard loaned the government millions of dollars to fund the war—which is widely recognized as the turning point that led to victory.

When Girard died, his estate was worth about $7.5 million, equivalent to about $50 billion today. The directives in his will were so clear that there were no changes in his instructions for over 120 years. His will left about $2 million to fund a school for orphans. Today, Girard College has a substantial endowment and continues to provide a university preparatory and secondary school education for economically disadvantaged children in a boarding school environment on forty-four acres in Philadelphia.

As most donors will not put together a will as thoughtfully as Girard, the gift agreement you help them to craft will ensure that their wishes are carried out for generations to come. After all, no one knows how to navigate the internal waters of your organization better than you do.

stories from the real world

Nonbinding Statement of Intent Template

Agreement to Establish the [NAME OF ENDOWED FUND]

at [YOUR CHARITY]

[Insert information about [YOUR CHARITY], when it was founded, and its mission. Also include a brief introduction of the donor and the donor's connection to your charity.]

[YOUR CHARITY] appreciates the philanthropic support of its donors that allow it to pursue its mission. To ensure that donors' gifts are used for the intended purpose, to allow [YOUR CHARITY] to plan effectively, and to comply with accounting and auditing requirements, [YOUR CHARITY] and its donors execute statements of intent.

[YOUR CHARITY] gratefully acknowledges the generosity of [NAME OF DONOR], who through this Statement of Intent commits to establishing the [NAME OF FUND] ("Fund"), at [YOUR CHARITY]. To protect the interests of both the Donor and [YOUR CHARITY], we agree as follows:

1. Donor's Commitment: The Donor is making a charitable gift of $[AMOUNT WRITTEN NUMBERICALLY] to [YOUR CHARITY], in the form of cash or readily marketable securities ("stocks"), according to the following schedule:

   [XX/XX/20XX] $[PAYMENT AMOUNT WRITTEN NUMERICALLY]

   [XX/XX/20XX] $[PAYMENT AMOUNT WRITTEN NUMERICALLY]

   [XX/XX/20XX] $[PAYMENT AMOUNT WRITTEN NUMERICALLY]

   Gifts of stock will be valued according to Internal Revenue Service guidelines in effect at the time the stock is transferred to [YOUR CHARITY]. Currently, these guidelines value the stock at the average of the high and low trades on the date of transfer to [YOUR CHARITY].

   The parties acknowledge that all or part of this nonbinding intention may be paid by a donor-advised fund or other third party. These assets are not the property of the Donor and are subject to the control and discretion of the sponsoring charity. The terms of this intention will be governed by [YOUR CHARITY'S HOME STATE] law.

2. [YOUR CHARITY'S] Commitment: In recognition of this generous commitment, [YOUR CHARITY] will create an endowed fund to be known as the [NAME OF ENDOWED FUND]. The purpose of the Fund is to provide financial support for [DESCRIPTION OF PURPOSE AND ANY RESTRICTIONS ON THE USE OF THE ENDOWED FUND].

3. Management of the Completed Gift: The [NAME OF ENDOWED FUND] will be pooled and invested with [YOUR CHARITY]'s other endowed funds in accordance with its regular investment and management policies. Net income from the Fund, as determined by application of [YOUR CHARITY]'s spending rule policy, as it may be amended from time to time, will be used according to the terms of Paragraph 2.

4. Planning for the Future: Endowment gifts are designed to last for all time. However, it is impossible to anticipate how changing circumstances may impact [YOUR CHARITY]'s ability to comply with all of the provisions of this Agreement. Accordingly, in the event future developments, including reputational risk, make it impracticable for [YOUR CHARITY] to carry out the specific terms of this Agreement, the president of [YOUR CHARITY] shall have the discretion, upon approval of [NAME OF GOVERNING BOARD] to rename and/or direct the use of the Fund for a purpose as close as possible to the Donor's original intent.

5. Recognition:

    a. The Donor will be referred to as [FORMAL NAME OF DONOR] in connection with this gift. This contribution [MAY or MAY NOT] be publicized in donor recognition vehicles produced by [YOUR CHARITY] or other entities, including print, spoken broadcast, and/or electronic media; and

    b. [YOUR CHARITY] will recognize the gift with an appropriate public announcement unless directed otherwise by the Donor.

_____   _____

[NAME OF DONOR]   Date
Donor

[YOUR CHARITY]

_____   _____

By: [NAME OF AUTHORIZED SIGNATOR]   Date

       [TITLE]

When Do I Need a Gift Agreement?

Gift agreements are required for:

◆ All gifts paid over more than one fiscal year (you should consider a pledge card for multiyear commitments with no detailed restrictions)

◆ All gifts subject to restriction

◆ Restricted commitments that will mature in the future but for which the donor wants certainty in how you will use the funds. These gifts include restricted gifts from the donor's will; restricted gifts from the donor's retirement plan (IRA, 401(k), etc.); and restricted gifts from the donor's life insurance proceeds

Should the Gift Agreement Be Binding or Nonbinding (Statement of Intent)?

Whether a gift agreement should be binding or nonbinding is a question for your legal counsel. As a general rule, most organizations prefer to use nonbinding statements of intent because they provide maximum flexibility to change the gift with no tax implications to the donor. An organization should almost always use a nonbinding statement of intent when:

◆ The donor intends to pay the gift commitment from a donor-advised fund (DAF)

◆ The donor may pay the gift commitment from a DAF or the donor's personal assets, but is unsure

◆ The donor may have the gift commitment paid by others (family members, friends, matching gift company)

Your organization may want to use a binding gift agreement if:

◆ You want to enforce the pledge against the donor or the donor's estate

◆ You want to borrow against the pledge (for larger organization, this includes bonding)

◆ You need to demonstrate the seriousness of your commitment to carry out the donor's wishes

◆ You need to ensure that the donor's estate is able to carry out the donor's wishes. Keep in mind that if a donor dies with an outstanding commitment to your organization, you will struggle to collect it from the estate unless you have a binding gift agreement in place

What Is a Binding Estate Agreement?

A binding estate agreement is a contract between your organization and the donor indicating that the donor will pay off a binding commitment from the donor's estate. It is usually used to ensure that the organization and the donor will meet their obligations after the donor has died. Binding estate agreements are only enforceable in some states.

Gift Agreement Process

The gift agreement process should be as simple or as complex as is required to meet the needs of your organization. As a general rule, all charities should have at least three gift agreement templates, covering binding, nonbinding, and estate gifts. For the most sophisticated organizations, we have helped create more than forty gift agreement templates. This is probably too many unless you work for an exceptionally large organization and the gift agreement templates will all be used on a regular basis. If in the future you determine that you are using additional forms on a regular basis (for example, for capital projects), you can create them. Because gift agreements are state-specific, it is best to have the templates drafted by your own legal counsel.

Estate Administration

Estate administration is the process of collecting gifts for your organization that have been left under a donor's will, living trust, retirement plan, life insurance policy, donor-advised fund, or other payable-on-death/transfer-on-death account. The goal is to ensure that you collect everything to which your organization is entitled as quickly as possible to carry out the donor's wishes.

Estate Administration Process and Procedures

The estate administration process will vary by state, but most states follow a similar set of steps to administer an estate. Your procedures should be designed to work with multiple states. The key to effective estate administration is to develop a time frame for each step and regularly follow up with the parties involved to hasten completion of the process.

My Donor Has Died—**Now What?**

It is always a sad day when you learn of the death of a loyal supporter of your organization. Notification of a donor's passing can come from a death notice in the newspaper, word of mouth, receipt of a notice of administration of estate, and, more recently, by a change in status or notice on a social networking site or tweet.

BEFORE YOU DO ANYTHING ELSE, independently verify that your donor has actually died by calling the funeral home, checking the Social Security Death Index, or by checking with members of the community who would know. You never want to wrongly contact the loved ones of your donor to express condolences only to discover that the donor is alive and well!

The first step for your organization is to send a hand-written note or card to the family of the deceased to express your sympathies. Each note should be custom tailored to the donor and the relationship the donor had with your organization and, in some cases, with you personally.

If the person was known by the board chair or the CEO, be sure that each of them also writes a personal note to the family. Most families are deeply appreciative when they receive multiple notes from an organization telling of the importance of the individual to the charity. Ideally, these notes will express your sorrow at their loss and how the donor will be missed but will live on through the donor's generosity to the charity. Including an outcomes-based story about the donor's philanthropy or an anecdote about his or her work with the charity will bring great comfort to the family at this difficult time. Be sure to sign the card with your full name and the name of your organization so the family is aware of its origin.

If the donor was particularly important, contact the family to determine how they want you to share the news with your other constituents. Many charities have an electronic newsletter that can share the sad news of the donor's passing, highlights of the donor's life, and information about burial and memorial services, as appropriate. It may seem like a modest gesture, but in smaller communities or for charities that engage multiple generations of a single family, these types of gestures show your true appreciation for the donor, provide comfort, and also help to ensure that you are not seen as only there when asking for a gift.

Notice of Administration or Probate

If your organization was named as the beneficiary of an estate or living trust, you will typically receive a Notice of Administration or Probate within thirty to sixty days of the donor's death. This notice normally comes from the estate attorney or the personal representative/executor. In the case of a living trust, the notice may be less formal since the court is not involved, and will be sent by the trustee of the trust.

When you receive the notice, it should include a copy of the will. If it does not, you should request one from the attorney or executor. If you encounter

---

Check with Legal Counsel

Donors may seek to negotiate the terms of their gift agreement. If you stray substantially from the form of gift agreement that has been drafted and preapproved by your legal counsel, be sure to pass the final draft of any completed gift agreement by counsel before execution by your donor.

observation

---

resistance to your request, it can be requested from the courthouse where it has been filed for probate. In the case of a living trust, you are not entitled to a copy of the document, but most trustees will provide you with at least a copy of the section pertaining to your organization.

To move the administration process forward, upon receipt of the notice, send a letter thanking the personal representative/executor/trustee/estate attorney ("executor") and providing the best contact information for your charity. Include with the letter your charity's complete legal name and address, a current and signed form W-9, and the determination letter from the IRS showing your tax-exempt status.

Occasionally, a donor will pass on who had informed you of a legacy gift and you will not receive any correspondence whatsoever. If it has been 120 days and you did not receive a notice, you should contact the family and ask about the estate administration. A phone call is always more personal and appropriate to handle delicate matters like this. Prior to asking about the intention, be sure to ask how the family is doing and if it needs assistance with estate administration. When you do open that part of the conversation, always lead with your desire to ensure that the deceased's wishes are carried out.

Open the File

With the notification in hand, you should open your estate file. Create and fill out an estate administration timeline and form to use as a checklist for administering the estate. If you are administering a large number of estates, have an electronic tracking system created that will automatically populate the due dates and reminders and feed your electronic to-do list or calendaring program so that you are sure to move forward proactively in each step of the estate administration process.

Be Patient, But Not Too Patient

Once an estate is open, the executor must inventory all of the assets, pay any outstanding debts, and liquidate assets before making distributions. In some cases, when it is clear that the estate is solvent (i.e., will have sufficient assets), the executor may elect to make interim distributions or make outright distributions to beneficiaries of specific amounts.

As a general rule, if your organization is to receive a specific bequest (either a specific dollar amount or a particular asset), you should receive it within twelve months, sometimes sooner. However, if your organization is to receive a percentage of what is left after everyone else has been paid (what is called a residuary bequest or interest), the timeline will be longer. Most estates will file an inventory within nine months since that is the deadline for filing the federal estate tax return. Even if the estate is not subject to federal estate tax, the estate will want to have completed the inventory before that time to document the fact that an estate tax return is not due.

Most states also have a state inheritance or estate tax, and the due date is frequently eight or nine months after the death of the donor. For that reason, if you do not have a copy of the inventory of the estate and a good estimate of your residuary interest, it is wise to write the executor and ask for one after ten months. The final distribution is usually within six months of the completed inventory unless there are illiquid assets, such as real estate or collectibles, that take longer to have appraised and sell.

Receipt and Release

Before receiving your distribution, the executor should provide you with a Receipt and Release to execute (sometimes called a Release and Refunding Bond). Other than the will, *this is the most important estate administration document* and one you should review carefully with your legal counsel if you are not familiar with it. The Receipt and Release generally states that your organization has received the funds (or a portion of the funds) it is entitled to from the estate and releases the executor from any liability for those funds. It can also include a provision requiring your organization to return the distribution if the estate runs out of funds and other beneficiaries or creditors are entitled to some of the funds.

The Distribution is Finally Here

While the loss of any donor is a time for reflection, the arrival of the estate distribution allows you to put the donor's generosity to work. Before you do, make sure that you send a note thanking the executor and attorney for their work on the estate and explain how the distribution will be used. At that point, process the gift as an estate gift received, record it in your database, and put the gift to work as designated by the donor. If the gift is not designated, your organization should have a policy for how undesignated estate gifts are used. Many organizations designate all unrestricted estate gifts to "Board Designated Endowment," keeping the principal intact and spending the earnings for an important purpose. This should be documented in your gift acceptance policy.

Closing the Estate File

Once the final distribution has been received, you should close the estate file. It is likely that your auditors will want to review the file during the audit of the fiscal year, so keep the closed file handy. Once the audit is complete, you should archive all closed estate files from the prior year for future reference.

My Best Two Years in Legacy Gifts

The best two years in legacy gifts for one of my employers were my first year and my last year. The last year resulted from growth in the program using many of the ideas in *Getting Started in Charitable Gift Planning* and this *Resource Book*. The first year was due to collection of millions of dollars in estate receivables that had been allowed to sit outstanding for several years.

—Brian

stories from the real world

Retirement Plans, Life Insurance Policies, and Payable-on-Death Accounts

Not all gifts from deceased donors will come from estates or living trusts. A wide variety of financial instruments can have beneficiary designations or be payable on death to your charity. In most cases, you will be designated to receive a set percentage of the remainder or the entire account. Distributions from these types of accounts should be completed very quickly. If your organization was known to be the beneficiary and you have not received any notice (or a check!) within three months, you should follow up directly with the financial institution involved. In some cases, if the executor has not provided the institution with an original death certificate, you may be required to produce one to make your claim.

Keep in mind that it is possible that donors could have changed their minds; it's possible that there will be no gift. It is more likely, however, that the account is sitting dormant and a gentle phone call or letter from you will get the responsible person to move forward on the distribution.

To Recap

◆ Gift planning infrastructure helps ensure that your program will be sustainable for the long term, starting with an internal case.

◆ Setting up gift counting, recognition, and acceptance policies *before* you are faced with actual gifts ensures that you set policies that will be sustainable for your organization and fair to your donors.

◆ Gift agreements document the understanding between your organization and your donors. Effective gift agreements protect these important relationships by clearly articulating the roles and responsibilities of both parties and stating the gift restrictions.

◆ Legacy gifts will take far longer to collect, and may not be received at all, without an effective, proactive estate administration process. Set up your procedures and forms up front and you will maximize realized legacy gift revenue for your organization.

Chapter Seven

Prospect Interaction

IN THIS CHAPTER

---→ What you should learn about a prospect

---→ Identifying clues to financial capacity

---→ Developing activity-tracking tools

---→ Building a robust gift planning stewardship program

In *Getting Started in Charitable Gift Planning,* we provided you with detailed information about integrating gift planning into your moves management system. In this chapter, we provide you with helpful tools and advice on actually conducting visit and stewardship activity.

The most frequently requested gift planning training topic is how to identify and qualify gift planning prospects. For some reason, people are just uncomfortable with who they should be talking to about gift planning and how to have that conversation. Fortunately, everyone, regardless of wealth, can be a gift planning prospect. As we noted earlier, however, it is possible to further refine that pool so that you are talking to the very best gift planning prospects. They are the individuals who are loyal to your organization. When you don't have a better way to measure loyalty, use consistency in giving as a proxy.

With those prospects identified, your next step is to put them into your moves management system so that you track your activity with them. And the very first thing you'll want to do is visit with them so you can learn more about their engagement with your organization and qualify them as gift planning prospects.

What You Should Learn About a Prospect

Once your organization has identified a potential gift planning prospect, the next step is to qualify the prospect. Qualification focuses on three fundamental questions: "What do we know about them? What is their relationship to the organization? What is their financial capacity to give?" Information you should garner through research, peer reviews, and qualification visits include:

Personal statistics:

◆ Spouse / significant other / length of relationship

◆ Parents / children / grandchildren / nieces / nephews / brothers / sisters

◆ Age / education / occupation / job history / professional-technical skills

◆ Travel / vacations / leisure activities / hobbies / intellectual interests

◆ Birthplace / where have they lived / family history

◆ Photographs / books / mementos /
awards / prized possessions

◆ Community, philanthropic, social involvement / interests

◆ Political, religious, cultural, professional affiliations

◆ Personality traits / likes / dislikes

◆ Physical health / disabilities

Relationship to organization:

◆ Donor / total gifts / largest gift / history of giving / types of gifts

◆ Volunteer work / positions held / history of involvement

◆ Friend / grateful patient / staff / family of patient / board member / volunteers / committee
member

◆ Invitations sent / events attended / mailings sent

◆ Telephone calls / visits / correspondence / meetings attended

◆ Specific programmatic interests / staff or
volunteer relationships

◆ Issues of concern / criticisms offered / suggestions made

◆ General areas of interest / requests for help or assistance

◆ Family's or friend's relationship to organization

Financial capacity:

◆ Cash (savings, checking, certificates of deposit, money market funds)

◆ Stocks / bonds

◆ Art / stamp / coin / jewelry / book collections

◆ Pension plans—IRA, 403(b), 401(k), annuities

◆ Real estate (home, condo, undeveloped land, second home, rentals)

◆ Automobiles (cars, trucks, motor homes, motorcycles), boats

◆ Insurance policies

◆ Furniture / furnishings (china, glassware, silverware, etc.)

◆ Business ownership / interests

Qualifying Visit Questions to Use with a Prospect

Ideally, you will already know the information outlined above through research and peer review when calling a prospect to ask for a qualifying visit. However, the reality of fundraising is that you will know almost none of this information and your responsibility on the qualifying visit will be to find out this information in a sensitive and appropriate way.

The following are examples of questions that will directly or indirectly lead prospects to share information, which could be helpful in determining their interest in gift planning:

Personal statistics:

◆ What do you/did you do for work?

◆ Where did/do your children attend college?

◆ What do your children do for a living?

◆ What ages are your children/grandchildren?

◆ What other charities are important to you?

◆ What volunteer activities do you perform?

◆ Where were you born/raised?

◆ What has happened to your neighborhood over the years?

◆ Where do you like to vacation?

◆ What are your plans for the holidays?

Relationship to organization:

◆ How/why did you get involved with our charity?

◆ What are some of the activities or events that you have been involved with?

◆ What have been your most positive experiences at our charity?

◆ Have any of your family members or close friends been involved with our charity?

Small Talk is Big!

You should learn more about the prospect in the small-talk, getting-to-know-you portion of the qualifying visit than in the formal conversation. Be purposeful with your questions even as you get to know someone's personal story. A simple question about a picture of a fishing trip on the wall can lead to valuable information about boat ownership, vacation homes, and areas of interest. I have often found that donors open up when the right open-ended questions are asked, allowing you to truly get to learn what is important to them.

—Robert

- What information do you receive from our charity? Is it helpful to you?

- What information could our charity provide that would be valuable to you?

- What are your long-term hopes for our charity and its mission?

- If there was one thing you could change about our charity today, what would it be?

- What do you think of the job the President and current Boards are doing?

Specific questions for educational institutions:

- How did our charity help lead to your success?

- Did you participate in any activities while a student?

- Describe your favorite moments as a student.

- Have you been back to campus recently?

- Do you read the magazine? What is your favorite part?

- Do you stay in touch with friends from your days as a student?

- Tell me about your favorite faculty member.

- What was your favorite class? Why?

Specific questions for healthcare organizations:

- How was your care at the hospital?

- Do you have a favorite doctor or staff person at the hospital?

- What do you consider to be quality health care?

- Which of our services do you use the most?

- If you were to tell others about your care at the hospital, how would you describe it?

Financial capacity:

- Tell me about your career. What do you do? How long have you been with them? How has the industry changed since you started?

- What was it like working for _____?

- I understand that you started your own business. How did you get started?

- Are these pictures of your children? Tell me about them. Where was this one taken? How old are they? Do you have any grandchildren?

- You mentioned that you like to travel. Where did you go this year? Who did you go with?

- If I wanted to reach you during the winter, do you have an alternative address, or are you here year-round?

◆ What are your interests outside of work? Do you have any hobbies?

◆ When you think about your life, what are your financial priorities?

◆ What do you think the market is going to do in the next year?

◆ Where do you get reliable information on financial, estate, and tax planning?

◆ What sort of retirement plan does a company like yours offer its employees?

◆ What strategies do you think are effective in helping parents plan for the cost of their children's college education?

◆ Do you support other charities in addition to our charity?

◆ How do you determine what level of support to make to charities?

◆ If we were to demonstrate our commitment to an area that is important to you, would you consider increasing your giving?

◆ Where does our charity fall on your list of charitable priorities?

Gift planning (generally not asked on the qualifying visit, unless the donor is very open and interested):

◆ Appreciated Stock

  ❖ Did you know that if you make a gift of appreciated stock instead of cash, you avoid the capital gain you would recognize on the sale? Even if you want to continue to hold the stock, you can donate it and then purchase new shares after a reasonable waiting period, increasing your cost basis.

  ❖ You mentioned that you are a VP at Whirlpool. Will the pending merger with Maytag have any tax implication for your stock holdings?

  ❖ (If a donor insists on making a gift today) I can't thank you enough for this tremendous commitment to our charity. When I come back to finalize the details of how you want to allocate the gift, I'll bring a colleague who specializes in putting together gifts to maximize the tax benefits for you.

◆ Closely-Held Business Interests / Partnerships / LLCs

  ❖ You mentioned that you are going to pass the business to your kids. Did you know there are some ways you can do that that will actually save you money on the transaction by being charitable? On my next visit, I'll bring our specialist in that area so we can talk about it in more detail.

  ❖ What does your business do? How is it structured? Is it difficult to get profits out due to tax concerns? Did you know there are some charitable solutions to help solve those problems?

◆ Alternative Investments

  ❖ Our charity invests a fair portion of its endowment in alternative investments. If you were interested in donating a portion of your interest, I could share the information with our

Treasurer's Office to see if it is something we could accept and hold in our portfolio until it matures.

◆ Qualified Plan/IRA Assets

> ❖ When most people consider a gift, they don't think about some of the assets in their portfolio that could help. Suppose, for example, you funded the scholarship now with $_____ to take advantage of the matching gift program, and then you brought it up to a full scholarship later by naming our charity as the beneficiary of your IRA? By giving the IRA to our charity instead of your kids, you avoid up to 70 percent tax due on the transfer to your children.

> ❖ You mentioned before that you are single. Who have you named to benefit from your IRA or life insurance provided by your employer? Did you know you can name our charity and become a member of the exclusive Legacy Society?

◆ Life Insurance

> ❖ Now that you've retired, do you have any life insurance policies you no longer need?

◆ Real Estate

> ❖ That's a great tan. Where did you go? Do you own a place there?

> ❖ Now that the kids are grown, will you be selling the house?

> ❖ With vacation properties difficult to sell, we have seen an increase in interest in giving these properties to our charity. Do you own any properties that you no longer use that might be suitable gifts?

◆ Tangible Personal Property

> ❖ What a collection of art! Can you show me your favorites? In what pieces are you disappointed?

> ❖ You've built up an amazing collection of Civil War items. Do your kids share your interest?

Clues of Financial Capacity

In addition to questions you might ask about financial capacity, there are frequently additional clues that your prospect will leave that demonstrate financial capacity. By paying attention to what you see and information that is volunteered, you can begin to form a financial picture of your prospect without asking any leading questions at all. Some clues to look for include:

◆ Donor writes checks from an investment management account

◆ There are brokerage statement envelopes on the hall table

> ### Just Let the Prospect Know
>
> If you are not the gift planner, notice that the questions do not "ask" if you can bring the gift planner on the next visit. Rather, they assume that you will. In our experience, if you ask permission, the answer will almost always be no. But if you say you are bringing the gift planner as part of your process, the prospect rarely objects. Use this approach to move the gift planning process forward.
>
>

◆ Has a close relationship with broker

◆ Has a close relationship with attorney and/or accountant

◆ Has a trust officer

◆ Complains of dividends going up or down

◆ Invests in tax-free bonds

◆ Is in the process of rewriting will

◆ Realizes that children are wealthy or "taken care of"

◆ Speaks of using annual gift tax exclusion

◆ Knows the estate or "death" tax rate

◆ Has family trusts and pour-over wills

◆ Holds real estate for investment purposes

◆ Has more than one home

◆ Likes a steady income

◆ Is planning for retirement

◆ Is approaching 59½ or 70½—IRA distribution periods

◆ Has a private/family foundation

◆ Sends gifts from a donor-advised fund

◆ Owns home outright

◆ Is not happy with will or estate plan

◆ Knows about the generation-skipping tax

◆ Is an owner of a closely-held company or a partnership

◆ Holds investments that were received as an inheritance or gift

◆ Worked for the same employer for majority of the person's career

◆ Subscribes to the Wall Street Journal or watches CNBC or Fox Business regularly

Track Your Activity

Your prospect database should have built-in reports to track visit activity, but may not effectively track gift planning results. The simple activity report below tracks how often gift planners discuss prospect strategy with other front-line gift officers, the number of legacy society asks by the fundraiser, and the number of new members in the legacy society. This data will allow you to track your activity and ensure that you are strategizing about legacy gifts and making legacy asks.

practical tip

Monthly Fundraiser Activity Report			
Month: July			
	Gift Planner One	Gift Planner Two	Gift Planner Three	Office Totals
Prospect Strategy Discussions With Front-Line Fundraisers			
This Month	2	5	4	11
Year-to-Date	19	41	12	72
By Fundraiser this Month			
Fundraiser 4	1	2	1
Fundraiser 5	1	1	0
Fundraiser 6	1	1	0
Fundraiser 7	2	1	0
Fundraiser 8	3	1	0
Fundraiser 9	2	1	0
Fundraiser 2	1	1	0
Fundraiser 1	2	1	0
Fundraiser 3	3	1	0

Legacy Society	Current Month	Year-to-Date	Campaign-to-Date
New Members	3	3	4
Qualifying Asks	36	80	80
Fundraiser 4	2	4	4
Gift Planner 2	1	5	5
Fundraiser 5	0	6	6
Fundraiser 6	4	7	7
Fundraiser 7	4	4	4
Fundraiser 8	8	9	9
Fundraiser 9	1	2	2
Fundraiser 10	0	5	5
Fundraiser 2	7	10	10
Fundraiser 1	5	6	6
Gift Planner 1	2	18	18
Fundraiser 3	2	4	4

Activity-Tracking Tools

As you complete your qualifying visits and other steps in your moves management process, it is important to track your activity in the prospect database and using tracking reports. Remember, if it is not in the database, it didn't happen!

Stewardship

Once you have moved your prospects through the moves management process and asked them for a legacy gift, you might think that your work is done. In fact, it is just the opposite. Because many legacy gifts are revocable and will not mature to your organization for many years, you need to do an exemplary job maintaining your organization's relationship with the donor to ensure that the gift is not removed from the donor's plans between the commitment and when the donor dies. It used to be that it was rare for a donor to remove an organization from the will or other legacy gift, but recent research from Russell James tells us that it is becoming far more common as older donors change their last will due to reasons such as:

◆ Changing interests

◆ They are no longer in charge of their own finances

◆ Assets are passed by contractual relationships (beneficiary of retirement plan, life insurance, payable/transfer-on-death accounts, etc.)

◆ Charities fail to stay in touch

You need to set up a strong system to steward your relationships—or risk losing the gifts.

In *Getting Started in Charitable Gift Planning*, we shared some core ideas for stewardship with the new generations of donors, including a strong story about the impact of your mission and the outcomes created by past planned gifts, the need for meaningful volunteer opportunities for younger donors, and the role of the seven touches philosophy in stewardship. For the balance of this chapter, we will provide you with tools you can use to implement these ideas, as well as the basic stewardship tools no planned giving program should be without.

Effective stewardship has three separate components: thanking, recognizing, and stewarding. It is vital for your organization to have a concrete plan in place for all three or you will not receive all of the legacy gifts that you have spent time developing.

Thanking

Thanking requires proper acknowledgment of donations of time, talent, and treasure, the three legs of donor participation. As with annual fund donors, legacy donors seek a contemporaneous thank-you at the time the donor informs your organization about the gift, indicating that you intend to use the gift where it will be directed, and then providing reports of the progress of that program for the duration of the donor's life. By connecting a legacy donor to the people at your organization who are providing the service to be funded or who benefit from it, legacy donors will feel secure that their gifts will come to good use. The thank-you process and the relationship that follows create a trust that your organization will use the gift as intended, even after the donor is not there to ensure that you do so.

Because legacy gifts will not mature until the future, legacy donors must feel confident that your board members are engaged and committed to the future. Each of your board members should be asked to join the legacy society to increase their visibility and investment in the organization. Board members should also be used in the thanking process. It is very powerful for a new legacy donor to receive a thank-you note or telephone call from a board member. It makes it clear that the gift is valued and far more likely that the gift will be used for its intended purpose.

Recognizing

Many charities struggle to effectively recognize legacy donors. Because these gifts usually do not mature until the future, there is often an element of "fairness" that comes into the conversation. Charities feel it is unfair to treat a legacy donor the same as a major donor since the gift from the legacy donor has not yet been irrevocably transferred to the charity.

However, as Penelope Burk points out in her seminal work *Donor-Centered Fundraising,* recognition and stewardship for major and annual donors are not a postgift activity but an investment in the *next* gift. The same holds true for legacy donors. The recognition and stewardship today are for the final gift—the one that comes when the donor passes.

The Role of the Donor Recognition Society

The legacy/recognition society is the most common method of recognizing legacy donors to your organization. It allows you to publicly recognize gifts that will not mature until the future, as well as to immortalize those who have died leaving legacy gifts. It honors those individuals who support your mission and love the organization enough to create a gift of great significance for it. The most common purposes for a donor recognition society are:

◆ Thanking and acknowledging gift planning donors, many of whom will not be alive when their gifts mature and come to benefit your organization

◆ Maintaining and strengthening the relationship of gift planning donors to your organization

◆ Providing a vehicle for ongoing communication with gift planning donors (stewardship)

◆ Engaging gift planning donors with the organization and its mission on an ongoing basis (stewardship)

◆ Focusing attention on the value of legacy gifts to your organization

◆ Encouraging others to consider and make legacy gifts

The Store-Front Pioneers

I recently worked with Finger Lakes Community College Foundation on building its legacy society. It did not have a single person or donor who had made a planned gift that warranted the naming of a legacy society. Undaunted, the staff and volunteers suggested that they name the society, "The Store-Front Pioneers." It turns out that the college was founded by local people who felt that their area needed a college. Rather than build a campus right away, they held their first classes in the vacant storefronts downtown. Eventually, the college grew and built its own campus, but everyone remembers the Store-Front Pioneers, what they did to establish the college, and the meaningful legacy their efforts have had for future generations in the Finger Lakes.

—Brian

Name and Branding

The name of your recognition society should be unique and clearly identifiable with your organization. Select a name that shares an important story about a legacy gift in your past, or a donor who made a legacy gift. If you do not have any such gifts, use a more generic name, but change it to something meaningful as soon as you can. Your society should have a brand or mark that complements and works in collaboration with your organization's existing brand using a symbol or mark, along with coordinating colors, look, feel, and design.

Membership Criteria

Membership in the legacy society should be extended to all individuals and their spouses who have:

◆ Set up an endowment to benefit your organization

◆ Included your organization in their estate plans

◆ Named your organization as a beneficiary of a trust, life insurance policy, charitable lead trust, payable/transfer-on-death account, donor-advised fund, or retirement plan, or

◆ Created a life-income gift (charitable remainder trust, pooled income fund, charitable gift annuity)

Membership Benefits

Membership benefits should be customized to combine thanking and recognizing your gift planning donors for their long-term commitment to your organization while showing them the long-term impact and outcomes created by their legacy gifts and those of others. Your organization needs to craft an *Acknowledgment and Recognition Plan* to articulate how you plan to steward these important donors. Some possible benefits of donor recognition society membership include:

◆ New members:

❖ Thank-you letter or personal thank-you call from Board President (or Chair)

❖ Thank-you letter from the CEO/President/Executive Director

❖ Certificate of Membership

❖ Memento (pin, paperweight, mug, clock, picture frame—it should not be an expensive item)

❖ Special mention in the annual report

◆ Existing Members:

❖ Listing in the annual report (before and after death-emeritus status)

❖ Invitation to recognition society event (written, followed up by personal invite from a Board member via telephone)

❖ Invitation to other special organizational events

❖ Special recognition at these other events (medallion, name tag ribbon, preferential seating, or parking)

❖ Personalized and hand-signed birthday card

   ❖ Personalized and hand-signed Thanksgiving Day/National Philanthropy Day card

   ❖ Annual phone call from Board member

◆ Deceased Members:

   ❖ Acknowledgment to family

   ❖ Collection of gift

   ❖ Funds put to purpose donor intended

   ❖ Recognition after death

   ❖ Ongoing connection with family to show long-term impact of gift (stewardship)

Stewarding

While your legacy society includes important elements of thanking, recognition, and stewardship, it is easy to slip into a pattern where you rely on it as your only stewardship mechanism. However, to be truly effective, stewardship should also include:

◆ Organizational commitment to relationship building and donor-focused fundraising through all employees and volunteers—stewardship is everyone's job

◆ Appreciation and fulfillment of the long-term outcomes your donors seek to create through their philanthropy

◆ Retention, renewal, and enhancement of your donors' support over a lifetime of giving and in perpetuity

Stewardship is the art of managing the relationship between your donors and your organization. A successful stewardship program will increase the connection with your most loyal legacy gift supporters, causing them to become more engaged with your mission and desiring to help fund impactful programs that further your success.

Stewardship Materials

To help you in your efforts, you should develop a multichannel marketing and outreach effort around stewardship. You will need to start using multimedia to illustrate the impact and outcomes of gifts. Web videos of interviews with donors and the individuals your charity serves, video conferencing between US-based donors and work being done overseas, webcams in remote locations where you are doing good work—these tools are available right now and connect donors to the work of your charity in a much more personal way than was possible even ten years ago. Using technology to reaffirm the results of your donors' philanthropy, or their future philanthropy, will go a long way toward ensuring that legacy gifts stay in place and current gifts are increased for the same purpose.

While it is important to use a broader range of technology, there are still some traditional tools that you need to have in place for your stewardship efforts, including a brochure, reply card, member roster, and information sheet.

Brochure and Reply Card

The legacy society brochure, which tells the story of the society and criteria for membership, remains a staple of every gift planning stewardship program.

Template Legacy Society Brochure Text

{Cover}

[NAME OF SOCIETY]

[LOGO OF SOCIETY]

{Page 1: Letter from the President or Board Chair}

"A man has made at least a start on discovering the meaning of human life when he plants shade trees under which he knows full well he will never sit." —Elton Trueblood

As I address these words to you, I feel I am talking to a friend and partner—one whose sense of stewardship for the future has led you to consider a legacy gift to [YOUR CHARITY].

I hope to soon be able to welcome you to the [NAME OF SOCIETY], whose members are esteemed at [YOUR CHARITY] not only for their powerful generosity but also for their vision and commitment. It is a special person indeed who is motivated to care so deeply and personally about the future of our organization.

As you consider a legacy gift, our team can help you explore the many ways you can meet your personal planning objectives while also achieving your charitable goals for [YOUR CHARITY].

Sincerely,

/s/

[SIGNATURE OF PRESIDENT OR BOARD CHAIR

{Page 2}

[INSERT STORY OF YOUR LEGACY SOCIETY NAMESAKE. IF NONE, INSERT INFORMATION ABOUT YOUR MISSION, ITS IMPORTANCE, AND HOW IT WILL BE REALIZED LONG TERM.]

{Page 3}

[NAME OF SOCIETY]

Established in [YEAR SOCIETY FORMED], the [NAME OF SOCIETY] honors the legacy and dedication of [NAMESAKE], whose vision for the future of [YOUR ORGANIZATION] continues to help us today. Membership in the Society is conferred upon individuals who have committed to the long-term future of [YOUR CHARITY] through a legacy or endowment gift.

Benefits of Membership

When you establish your legacy gift or endowment, you join a select group of individuals who have expressed an enduring commitment to [YOUR CHARITY]. As such, you are invited to exclusive gatherings throughout the year, including the annual [NAME OF SOCIETY] Luncheon. You will also receive a commemorative certificate and membership pin recognizing the lasting bond of your philanthropic support. Above all, you will have the certainty of knowing that your gift will continue to enhance [YOUR CHARITY'S] tradition of excellence while providing for the future.

[IF AVAILABLE, INSERT A QUOTE FROM YOUR NAMESAKE OR ABOUT YOUR NAMESAKE OR HOW THE GIFT FROM THE NAMESAKE MADE A DIFFERENCE.]

{Page 4}

Please Join Us

[YOUR CHARITY] encourages you to help build upon our accomplishments through membership in the Society. If you have included [YOUR CHARITY] in your plans or created an endowment for its support, you qualify for membership. Qualifying legacy gifts include creating an endowment or naming [YOUR CHARITY] as a beneficiary of your:

- Will or living trust

- Retirement plan

- Life insurance policy

- Payable/transfer-on-death account or

- Donor-advised fund

Also qualifying are individuals who set up other planned gifts such as:

- Charitable gift annuities

- Pooled income funds

- Charitable remainder trusts or

- Charitable lead trusts

For more information about membership in the [NAME OF SOCIETY] or to learn more about how you can establish your own legacy, please return the enclosed reply card or contact our [INSERT MAILING ADDRESS, PHONE NUMBER, EMAIL AND WEBSITE].

Reply Card Language for Society Brochure

(fold over card to be placed inside a reply envelope)

{Front of card}

_____Society (with branding and logo)

The _____ Society gratefully recognizes our closest friends who have generously committed to _____'s future through a legacy or endowment gift.

{Inside}

Thank you for considering a legacy gift to benefit _____.

If you have already included _____ in your plans, we are pleased to add you as a member of the _____ Society. Please complete the following information:

I/We wish to be:

☐ Referred to as: _____

in any recognition materials

☐ Anonymous members of the _____ Society

☐ Include my spouse _____as _____ Society member

{Back of Card}

_____
Name

_____
Address

_____
City, State, ZIP

_____
Email

Phone_____

The brochure invites the reader to join the society. It then uses a series of design elements to:

◆ tell the story of the naming of the society

◆ explain why legacy gifts, and the prospect's legacy gift, would be so important to the organization

◆ explain what constitutes a legacy gift that qualifies for membership

◆ make a call to action

The text of the brochure should be pithy and to the point, using quotes for a peer-to-peer ask component.

Note that the call to action provides multiple ways to contact a real person about a legacy gift, including a confidential reply card. The reply card for the brochure should be far less detailed than other print materials you might create, since the focus of this brochure is to invite individuals to join your legacy society. It only asks for what you need to take the next step with the prospect.

Welcome Letter and Information Sheet

All individuals who inform your organization about a legacy gift are automatically included in your legacy society, unless they opt out. However, just because we put them in the society does not mean that you do not want to know more about their legacy gift. The welcome letter and information sheet is a way for you to encourage members to share more information about their legacy gift in a nonthreatening way.

[NAME OF SOCIETY] Membership Form

Name: _____

Address: _____

Phone Number: _____

Email Address: _____

☐ I/We wish to be referred to as _____ in any donor recognition materials. Date of Birth: _____

☐ Include my spouse _____ as a member. Date of Birth: _____

☐ I prefer to remain anonymous and do not wish to be recognized publicly at this time.

Optional information to help us plan for the future:

I/We are pleased to acknowledge that I/we have named [YOUR CHARITY] as a beneficiary in my/our:

☐ Will/Living Trust

☐ Retirement Plan

☐ Life Insurance Policy

☐ Payable/Transfer-on-Death Account

☐ Donor-Advised Fund

☐ Charitable Remainder Trust

☐ Charitable Gift Annuity

☐ Pooled Income Fund

☐ Other _____

My gift is:

☐ Unrestricted

☐ Designated specifically for: _____

☐ Not yet determined. Please contact me to discuss options.

The estimated value of my gift is:

☐ $_____

☐ _____ percent of my estate, currently valued at $_____, for [YOUR CHARITY]

☐ _____ percent of my retirement plan/life insurance, currently valued at $_____, for [YOUR CHARITY]

Membership Roster

One of the key elements of effective recognition is the creation of a membership roster for the legacy society. It says to your donors that their gifts are important and you are telling the world that their gifts are important.

Charities create membership rosters in many different ways. Some have patio pavers with the names of all current and deceased members. Others use a donor wall in a prominent location at the charity.

As with so many things, ask your donors what works best for them. A short survey of members about recognition will tell you a great deal about what members want in recognition and how to use recognition to appeal to potential legacy donors.

Keep in mind the recognition profiles. Some donors will want no recognition and others will want to remain anonymous. Unless you have a large percentage of these types of donors, ignore those responses and create the roster based on the response of those individuals who want to be recognized.

Newsletter

While prospect newsletters have lost their efficacy for attracting new gift planning prospects (the response rates have fallen through the floor), the newsletter can be a useful tool for staying in touch with your society members, provided you have enough of them. You should send the newsletter to all existing members, plus anyone who has inquired about a legacy gift in the last five years.

The purpose of the newsletter is to stay in touch and share value information, not to solicit. It may result in new gifts, but if you try to do too much in one newsletter (identifying, cultivating, soliciting, and stewarding), it will lose effectiveness. Use the newsletter as a stewardship tool and it will serve you well.

Some items you should include:

◆ Donor profiles showing the impact and outcome of gifts, as well as donor motivations to make gifts; do not highlight how gift vehicles or tools work

◆ Articles that are generally helpful to your donors around financial planning

◆ "Letters to the Editor" section

◆ Tax law updates

◆ Information on who to contact on your staff if donors need assistance

If you do not have at least a few hundred people on the mailing list, designing and mailing a newsletter may be prohibitive. Instead, consider a personalized insider letter from someone at your organization who is well respected. Donors love to receive inside information right from the source. Such a letter will be an excellent substitute for the newsletter and easier to create. If budget is a problem, these materials can be sent electronically, but a print piece still produces better results.

Stewardship Events

Your legacy society should have one signature recognition event each year. It provides your members with an opportunity to meet and greet with your leadership, hear more about the organization's direction going forward, and assure them that their legacy gifts will be used wisely. Note that this is not a fundraising event, it is a stewardship event. There should be no solicitations of any type, be it an outright ask, silent auction, annual appeal, etc. The purpose of the event is to thank. If you also ask, then it dilutes the appreciation you convey for what these donors have already done for you.

For those who cannot attend, summarize those points with photos in your newsletter. To maximize the effectiveness of the event, include these elements:

◆ Held at a location where you can provide real-life examples of the benefits that matured gifts have produced

◆ Lunch (even though your society will have individuals of many different ages, the more-senior folks tend to attend these events and do not want to fight rush hour traffic and don't want to drive in the dark)

◆ Valet parking

◆ Speaker with a compelling message of the impact and outcomes of legacy gifts on the organization

The next generations of donors want to know that their gifts will be put to good use, as they intend, and the only way to show them this is to highlight matured gifts at your events.

Venue

Selecting an appropriate venue will make your entire event run more smoothly. The event should accommodate an older constituency with handicap-accessible ramps, a large number of bathrooms close by, coat checking, and adjacent or valet parking. Use outdoor and indoor signs to direct people to your event.

Ideally, the venue will be a location where you can showcase matured planned gifts to show the society members the good that has come from previous donors' planned gifts. (This will cultivate your donors' sense of "immortality" through their giving by suggesting you will honor them in the same way after they are gone.)

Scheduling

Set the time (ideally lunch or an afternoon tea) and date for your event as soon as you can, ideally at least one year ahead so you can announce it at this year's event. As soon as you set the date and time, put it on your website and any social media sites you offer. Send a "save the date" card, use a calendaring service to get the word out, and email at least three months ahead so that people put it on their calendars.

Event Stages

Your event should have several stages:

◆ Welcome: Attendees arrive, are issued name tags, and coats are hung. They are directed to a social area to meet with other members as well as your guest speaker and board members. This social time will be the most enjoyable for most of your society members, so allow sufficient time for it. (For example, if you schedule the event for noon, do not start serving the actual lunch until 12:30 p.m.) If you expect an older audience, chairs will be very important for this part of the event.

◆ Visiting at Tables: Allow people to visit at their dining tables before starting the formal program. Generally, twenty minutes or so is enough to get the food out and for people to connect. Do not leave seating to chance—assign seats. Be sure to put at least one board or staff member at each table with your donors. If you can put beneficiaries of your service (e.g., a scholarship student for a college society event) at each table, this adds great "outcomes" value.

◆ Formal Program: As dessert and coffee are served, the formal program can begin. It should not last more than twenty to thirty minutes. When the speakers have concluded, the event is over. For a noon event, the program should end by 1:30 p.m.

Menu

Your menu should include vegetarian and nonfish options to accommodate your guests. Because this will likely be an older group, plated food with wait staff is preferable to a buffet. Note that because this is a thank-you event, guests should not be charged to attend.

Room Setup

Ahead of the event, review the room and set up to meet the needs of your guests. The venue should be able to help with room diagrams. You may need to order a projector, lectern, and microphone. Even the best speakers should use the microphone for this event, since the audience may have hearing difficulties. When possible, consider setting up the room so as few people as possible have their backs to the podium, as it can be awkward to turn a chair around.

Invitations

As this is an important event, you should create an appropriate invitation. Have it printed on card stock and mailed in a proper envelope.

Your invitation list should include all members of the society and their family members. Since legacy gifts often impact inheritance for other family members, allow them to bring family members to your event. Also, include your board members and senior leadership if they are not already members. Society members want access to your senior leadership, so putting them in the room for your event will show the importance of legacy gifts.

You can follow up the invitation with an email about three weeks later to prompt people who have not responded to encourage them to come. We have also found it helpful to call the remaining nonresponders to invite them and offer rides. This should be done by a fundraiser or volunteer, not secretarial staff. If you reach the person, you want them to know that you personally want them to attend. They will be impressed that you actually called them yourself. If you cannot do this yourself, ask some of your volunteers to call to make the invitation.

The day before the event, consider having a group of volunteers call all of those who responded "yes" and confirm their attendance. That way you will limit the number of "no shows" and keep your costs down.

Giveaway Item

Attendees have come to expect some type of giveaway. It needs to be valuable enough to not appear cheap, but not so expensive that it appears you are wasting valuable resources. Ideally, it will be something that they can display at home or in the office that has your organization's name on it and will start a conversation about your charity.

Make sure you give yourself enough preparation time to find the item, order it, have it personalized, and have it delivered for the event. Remember, delicate objects can be beautiful, but easily broken. Nothing will put a crimp in your event like a giveaway that has been smashed. So keep "durability" among your criteria.

Program

No event is complete without an effective and enjoyable program. The program should not be long, but needs to include several key elements:

◆ Thanking donors for their legacy gifts

◆ Honoring members who died in the past year

◆ Sharing information about the outcomes created by past legacy gifts

◆ Inducting new members into the society

Thanks to donors should be made by either the president or the board chair. Reading the list of those members who have passed can be completed by the chair of your society, a member of the board, or a chaplain if your organization has one.

The guest speaker should be someone who can connect the planned gift to the venue of the event. If you could not find such a venue, then the speaker should be someone who can inspire your audience in less than ten minutes, and include at least one legacy gift outcome story in the process.

Induction of new members can be done by the president or board chair and yourself. Be sure to have a photographer present to memorialize the moment as you induct new members. You can send your new members framed photos of their induction to display in their homes or offices. With the program complete, thank your members and end the event.

If your society includes individual born after 1964 (Generation X and Millennials), you should consider a two-part event. Start first thing in the morning with a volunteer component, where all members of the society are invited to help with a service project directly related to your mission. For the Gen X and Millennials in the society, this type of volunteer opportunity will be much more engaging than just a luncheon.

Follow the service project with the lunch described above, allowing people to RSVP for just the service project, just the lunch, or both. Obviously, the lunch will be a less-formal affair than it might otherwise be (people staying through won't be in business attire), but it is a way to engage both audiences and not take on an additional event. Add to the lunch a report on the service project, including how many participated, what it accomplished, and how it will help your organization long term.

To Recap

◆ Interactions with prospects provide a great opportunity to learn about their affinity and financial capacity, using open-ended questions and small talk.

◆ By tracking your activity with prospects, you help to ensure that you move them through your moves management process and ask them to consider legacy gifts.

◆ An effective stewardship program includes thanking, recognizing, and stewarding.

◆ Your stewardship materials should be multichannel but still need to include an appropriate legacy society brochure, follow-up materials, and donor profiles.

◆ Your organization should host at least one stewardship event focused just on legacy society members each year. If the society includes members born after 1964, consider a two-part event that includes a service project in the morning, followed by lunch, to create a volunteer opportunity for younger members.

Chapter Eight

Marketing

IN THIS CHAPTER

- ···➔ One-on-one visits are best
- ···➔ Creating a gift planning marketing plan
- ···➔ Developing a gift planning marketing grid
- ···➔ Using a gift planning marketing tracking report

In *Getting Started in Charitable Gift Planning,* we provided information about building an effective gift planning marketing effort to meet the needs of principal prospects, major prospects, loyals, and "everyone else"—the four layers of the gift planning marketing pyramid. We noted that gift planning marketing to principal and major prospects is largely completed in one-on-one visits and conversations rather than through traditional marketing channels. The focus of your gift planning marketing efforts should be on your identified loyal prospects and those who are engaged by your mission, but might not be on your proactive marketing list because they are not readily identifiable.

To implement the marketing effort, we recommend three key tools: the gift planning marketing plan, grid, and tracking report.

The marketing plan is your detailed roadmap covering each and every step you will take in marketing gift planning over a three-year period. You may not implement the entire plan at once, but by planning for multiple years you ensure that your program will have continuity and growth over time.

The marketing grid is a quick, one-page summary that allows you to see what you need to accomplish each month to keep the plan on track. It is an invaluable tool for marketing management.

The final tool, the tracking report, is your scorecard. It helps you to evaluate the efficacy of your marketing plan and eliminate items that don't work and increasing your reliance on items that do. You'll want a five-year tracking report to ensure that you are measuring both short- and long-term success of your gift planning marketing effort.

Gift Planning Marketing Plan

The first step in communicating about your gift planning program is to have a plan. Most charities skip this step and use "random acts of marketing." This means that every once in a while they decide to send out a marketing piece related to gift planning. Unfortunately, this does not produce results. Instead, draft a plan based on your organization's moves management platform. Each marketing piece should help move prospects forward through your moves management steps.

To assist you in creating your own marketing plan, we have included a sample plan created for a fictional university. Note how the plan uses the different moves management steps of education, identification, cultivation, solicitation, and stewardship to move potential prospects along and eventually ask them for gifts. For each plan item, clear expectations are set for the purpose, content, audience, schedule, budget, and measures of success. In this way, you assure that whenever you spend valuable time and resources on marketing, there is a plan for how it moves prospects forward and how the individual piece will be measured.

Sample Donor-focused Gift Planning Marketing Plan

Summary: The Office of Gift Planning is a central unit within the Institutional Advancement Division of GPD University (GPD), providing philanthropic planning services to central development and all of the colleges, university centers, and programs that make up the university. It assists alumni, parents, and friends of the university in integrating their charitable intentions with their overall tax, estate, and financial planning. Our values-based, donor-focused approach ensures that goals are achieved today and in the future.

Philosophy: Marketing gift planning for GPD encompasses all outreach efforts and communications in the arena of structured outright gifts, life-income gifts, and estate commitments to GPD. Marketing communications are intended to:

- Educate the entire GPD constituency about gift planning opportunities

- Identify prospects within the GPD constituency who may have a particular interest in gift planning

- Cultivate relationships with those who express an interest in gift planning

- Solicit identified prospects through various media

- Negotiate gifts through fulfillment materials

- Steward donors who have made endowment, life-income, and estate commitments to GPD

Our ultimate goal is to increase long-term financial resources for GPD by providing outstanding service to prospective donors, their advisors, and our GPD colleagues. Initiatives are strategically timed throughout the year, organized around donors' timing, and significant university events.

The plan is based on a moves management platform and includes customized marketing for each unit that makes up the university. The program is designed to maintain a steady stream of communications and achieve consistency in message through content and visual identification, even while customizing for each unit.

All marketing communications will encourage prospects to "self-identify" by presenting a compelling message and contact information or a private (sealable) reply mechanism.

   I.   Educational Materials

      A. General Education—Communications to broad university constituencies using gift planning messages to create awareness

         1. GPD University Magazine

- Purpose: With a readership circulation of forty thousand, these advertisements serve to raise awareness, generate interest, and compel action

- Content: Full-page, four-color ads positioned on the inside back cover or in the "class notes" section, featuring a donor/student profile to show impact and outcomes; use QR codes to link readers back to the mobile website for gift planning content

- Audience: All alumni, friends, and students who receive the magazine

- Schedule:

Schedule:	Topic	Profile
Winter-DATE	Crafting Your Legacy-Wills	TBD
Spring-DATE	Crafting Your Legacy-Retirement Plans	TBD
Summer-DATE	Crafting Your Legacy-Life Insurance/DAFs	TBD
Fall-DATE	Crafting Your Legacy-Wills	TBD

- Budget: $0

- Measure: Number of self-replies and traffic at website

2. Existing Alumni Office monthly email newsletter (other newsletters TBD)—tip of the month

   - Purpose: Keep gift planning information in front of readers' minds

   - Content: Short segment each month, appropriate to the planning process, to drive traffic to the website through a hot link

   - Audience: All alumni

   - Schedule: Monthly

   - Budget: $0

   - Measure: Traffic at website

3. Existing newsletters

   - Purpose: Raise awareness, generate interest, and compel action

   - Content: Donor-focused advertisements profiles of students and coaches to show impact and outcomes tied to a donor-focused gift planning opportunity

   - Audience: Newsletter target audience

   - Schedule: Every other month

   - Budget: $0

   - Measure: Number of phone and email responses; traffic at website

4. Website/Media:

- Purpose: Provide an interactive on-line source of information

- Content: Purchased from Virtual Giving and modified to our mission

- Audience: All alumni, parents, and friends

- Schedule: Complete updates to donor stories quarterly

- Budget: $4,000 per year

- Measure: Number of unique visitors per month; time on page; number of pages visited; most common downloads; most commonly visited pages

B. Professional Advisors

1. Council

   - Purpose: Bring together up to twenty-four professional advisors closely affiliated with GPD's gift planning program to provide help for complex gifts, a referral network for top prospects, drafting for materials/steering committee for the Professional Advisors Network, and encourage gift planning generally

   - Audience: Advisors from each of the major professions

   - Schedule: Meet up to four times per year on campus to discuss tax law changes and other issues impacting charitable gift planning (February, June, September, November)

   - Budget: $1,000

   - Measure: Attendance at quarterly meetings and production of materials for Professional Advisors Network

2. Professional Advisors Network

   - Purpose: Provide gift planning information to professional advisors with a connection to GPD to encourage them to:

     o Make gifts of their own

     o Encourage clients to do so (40 percent of all life-income gifts are recommended by advisors)

     o Serve as a referral source for prospects who need advisors

     o Serve as a resource to draw upon for state-specific questions

   - Content:

     - Notebook of materials to include:

- General GPD information and giving opportunities

- Donor, faculty, and student profiles

- Descriptions of personal planning objectives and tools available to help meet them

- Sample bequest language

- Technical information on gift and estate tax implications of gift types

- Contact information for Office of Gift Planning

- Information on accessing a social network of attorneys affiliated with GPD

- Audience: All professional advisors in greater Philadelphia area and all GPD professional advisors nationally

- Schedule: Update materials every July

- Measure: Number of new members

C. University Community—Education programs designed for staff and volunteer leadership

1. Orientation

- Purpose: Training for new calling officers as they are hired

- Content: An introduction to marketing materials and the services offered by gift planning

- Audience: All new calling officers

- Schedule: Within one month of hire (one-on-one sessions with gift planner)

- Budget: $0

- Measure: Percentage of new gift officers trained

2. Donor-Focused Gift Planning Training

- Purpose: Training to introduce new donor-focused gift planning model

- Content: Framework of donor-focused gift planning and how to effectively leverage resources of Office of Gift Planning

- Audience: All calling officers at all levels, including president and senior management

- Schedule: One-time training—September 21 (1.5 hours)

- Budget: $0

- Measure: Participation

3. Leadership gift and major gift officer training

    - Purpose: Training program to assist calling officers at the bottom and middle levels of the giving pyramid to identify prospects who are ready for the gift planning discussion

    - Content: How to recognize gift planning opportunities and introduce the gift planning process into fundraising calls

    - Audience: Annual fund and major gift officers

    - Schedule: Five, half-day sessions each year, repeated on an annual basis—First Monday of January, March, June, September, and November

    - Budget: $10,000

    - Measure: Percentage of gift officers trained

4. President, senior management, deans, and principal gift officer training (PRN Training)

    - Purpose: Training program for those working with the university's highest level prospects to understand the gift planning process

    - Content: How to integrate prospects' philanthropic goals and objectives into their overall tax, estate, and financial planning

    - Audience: President, senior management, deans, and principal gift officers

    - Schedule: Two-hour training sessions once per calendar quarter, repeated on an annual basis—First Monday of January, March, September, and November

    - Budget: $8,000

    - Measure: Percentage of target audience trained

5. Board of Trustees training

    - Purpose: Training program for the board to educate trustees on how to introduce the gift planning process

    - Content: How the long-term goals of the university lend themselves to the gift planning discussion; review of case for legacy giving

    - Audience: Board of Trustees

- Schedule: One-hour training session once per calendar year, repeated on an annual basis—May board meeting

- Budget: $2,000

- Measure: Percentage of board members who join society

6. Parents' Council training

- Purpose: Training program for Parents Council on how to introduce the gift planning process

- Content: How the long-term goals of the university lend themselves to the gift planning discussion; review of case for legacy giving

- Audience: Parents' Council

- Schedule: One-hour training session once per calendar year, repeated on an annual basis—October meeting

- Budget: $2,000

- Measure: Percentage of Parents' Council who join society

II. Prospect Identification

A. Audience Selection

- Purpose: Create the initial list of prospects most open to a gift planning message

- Method: Review the database to find donors who have given:

  - 15 or more years

  - 10 of the last 15 years

  - 7 of the last 10 years

  - 5 of the last 7 years

  - 3 of the last 5 years

  Add to that list, to the extent that they are not already included, those who have made some gifts and are:

  - Current or former society members (or have informed us they have set up legacy gifts for GPD or another organization)

  - Individuals who have expressed an interest in gift planning with GPD in the past by returning a reply card or other device

- Current and/or former board members

- Current and/or former staff members

- Long-term volunteers

- Tied to GPD long term through personal or family associations

- Strong in philosophical or religious belief in helping others or in giving back

- Others who are strongly tied to our mission in a meaningful way

Together, this group represents those who believe closely in GPD and will support us financially. They are the most open to a gift planning message and providing long-term support.

Create the following rating system on the database:

Rating	Description
1	Known legacy gift donors
2	Prospects who have inquired about gift planning in the past but not captured in rating 1
3	Donors who have given 15 or more years not captured in ratings 1 and 2
4	Donors who have given 10 of the last 15 years not captured in ratings 1-3
5	Donors who have given 7 of the last 10 years not captured in ratings 1-4
6	Donors who have given 5 of the last 7 years not captured in ratings 1-5
7	Donors who have given 3 of the last 5 years not captured in ratings 1-6
8	Current or former board members not captured in ratings 1-7
9	Long-term volunteers and those tied to GPD long term through personal or family associations but not captured in ratings 1-8
10	Current or former staff members with at least some giving history, but not captured in ratings 1-9
11	Donors and prospects previously rated 1-10 but who fall off the rating system when ratings are reviewed (typically every other year)
12	Donors who have turned down legacy gift asks, but really are saying "not now" (qualified prospects)
13	Do not solicit for future gifts (prospects that have been identified and qualified, but it is clear they will never make a legacy gift)

- Schedule: Complete by July 31

- Budget: $0

- Measure: Number of qualified prospects in pool

B. Audience Segmentation—Begin the process of identifying donors in specific generational cohorts, target groups (married no children, single, women, those using "Miss," parents, grandparents) for messaging future communications.

- Schedule: Complete by December 31

- Budget: $0

- Measure: Number of prospects in each discreet group

C. Prospect Survey

- Purpose: Encourage previously identified gift planning pool to express an interest in estate planning, allowing GPD to pursue them immediately

- Content: Electronic and print survey covering estate planning and questions typically asked on a first visit; provide Estate Information Organizer as the thank-you for completing the survey (can also point them to the "Estate Planning Wizard" on the website)

- Audience: All gift planning prospects ranked 2-12

- Schedule: Send to a modest group each month to allow staff to respond in a reasonable period of time, start September 1

- Budget: TBD (depends on number of identified prospects)

- Measure: 7-8 percent response rate

D. Tell Your Story Campaign

- Purpose: Encourage existing legacy gift and endowment donors to tell why they elected to make their gift; provides university with good stories to tell and identifies donors who are likely willing to make another gift to add to their existing gift; also serves a stewardship purpose

- Content: Simple mail and electronic request with form to fill in and return

- Audience: All gift planning prospects rated 1

- Schedule: Start July 1

- Budget: $2,500

- Measure: Number of responses (expect 5 percent response rate)

E. Telephone Calling Program

- Purpose: Identify prospective prospects from the gift planning pool who respond to a phone call, allowing GPD to pursue legacy gifts immediately

- Content: Phone calls to inquire about gift planning interest

- Audience: All gift planning prospects rated 2-12 who have not responded to a gift planning mailing in the last three years

- Schedule: Start January 1

- Budget: TBD (need proposals from vendors)

- Measure: Number of responses

III. Cultivation

A. Brochure program

1. General brochure

   - Purpose: Leave-behind piece for calling officers

   - Content: Four-color brochure on gift planning; delivers a comprehensive but generalized description of all gift planning options as well as motivation, impact, and outcomes

   - Audience: Identified prospects for visits or who request information on multiple gift planning options

   - Schedule: Complete by September 1

   - Budget: $7,500 (depends on number printed)

   - Measure: Number used

2. Society brochure/membership roster (2 versions)

   - Purpose: Welcomes new members, thanks them, and explains the benefits of membership

   - Content: Printed brochure (reprinted annually); lists all members, provides information on the origins of the society, member benefits, and its importance within the university; include sample language

   - Audience: New society members

   - Schedule: Annually each fall

   - Budget: $1,000

   - Measure: None

B. University Reply Cards/College Reply Cards

- Purpose: Reply mechanism designed to produce responses

- Content: Consistent language across the university, matched to the fulfillment pieces created for gift planning purposes

- Audience: Entire population

- Schedule: For Gift Planning mailings—complete by July 1; for all other college and university cards—share new language by April 30 for inclusion in materials for the coming fiscal year

- Budget: $500

- Measure: Number of gift planning responses on reply cards

IV. Solicitations

    A. Postcard solicitation program

- Purpose: Solicit prospects to request information on gift planning or make a legacy gift

- Content: Five postcards per year. The front of each card will have a student/faculty photo and a story about outcomes. The back of each card will tie that story to a gift planning opportunity and include a reply device/unique URL/QR code for responses

- Audience: Gift planning prospects rated 1-12

- Schedule:

Schedule:	Topic
September	Beneficiary Designation—Wills
November	IRA Charitable Rollover/Year-End Appreciated Stock (split card)
January	Beneficiary Designations—Retirement Plans
March	Beneficiary Designations—Life Insurance/DAF
May	Beneficiary Designations—Wills

- Budget: TBD based on vendor/internal cost; number to mail

- Measure: Expect 0.5 percent response rate

    B. Email follow up to postcard program

- Purpose: Increase yield from postcard mailings

- Content: Reminder about postcard and link to website with more information on the topic

- Audience: Same as postcard

- Schedule: Same as postcard

- Budget: $0

- Measure: Open and click-through rates

C. Proposal packages

- Purpose: Create a standard printed and electronic proposal package as a response device to each type of gift planning inquiry, so support team can assist with fulfillment and to ensure consistency of information and disclosures

- Content: Letter, description of gift type, corresponding disclosure statement, calculations page, and appropriate insert or brochure packaged in a branded gift planning folder or appropriate email device

- Audience: All responders

- Schedule: Complete by July 1

- Budget: $0

- Measure: Completed gifts

D. General Contact Information

- Purpose: Make it easy for prospects and donors to reach the Office of Gift Planning

- Content: Toll-free telephone number and general gift planning email box such as giftplanning@GPD.edu

- Audience: Responders to all marketing

- Schedule: Completed by June 30

- Budget: $400 for the toll-free number

- Measure: Increased overall response rates

V. Stewardship

A. Update membership criteria—Membership is currently offered to individuals who name GPD as a beneficiary of a will, living trust, life insurance policy, retirement plan, charitable remainder trust, charitable gift annuity, or pooled income fund. Broaden membership to include anyone who has set up a gift that matures in the future or lasts in perpetuity (an endowment), i.e. a legacy gift.

- Schedule: Complete by July 31

- Budget: $0

- Measure: Number of new society members

B. Profile society donors more broadly in university and college-based publications—Donor profiles are the best way to steward donors while also encouraging others to consider similar gifts. Select a wide range of donors—young, middle age, older, and deceased. Highlight the impact and outcomes that their gifts achieved and why those were important to the individual or family. Tie this to the personal history or motivation of the donor and students who benefitted or will benefit from these gifts.

- Schedule: Ongoing; start by September 30

- Budget: TBD

C. Survey of society members

- Purpose: Confirm existing members, gain insight into their gift intentions, ask if we can count gifts that qualify and we have not counted to date, and start a dialog for further cultivation and stewardship

- Content: Letter and survey asking for permission to use name and asking for details/confirmation of qualifying gift

- Audience: Endowment, life-income, and estate gift donors (legacy donors)

- Schedule: Complete by August 30

- Budget: Estimated at $400

- Measure: Confirm 80 percent of members

D. Select a volunteer chair for society

- Purpose: Volunteer to sign letters and serve as an advocate/face of gift planning among the alumni

- Content: N/A

- Audience: Societies

- Schedule: As needed

- Budget: $0

- Measure: N/A

E. Society brochure/membership roster (two versions) (see also Cultivation section for cultivation purpose)

- Purpose: Steward existing society members

- Content: Lists all members, provides information on the origins of the society, member benefits, and its importance within the university; needs to tell a great story for both societies

- Audience: Existing society members

- Schedule: Annual

- Budget: $500

F. Benefits of membership

- Donor recognition lists

  o Purpose: Honor existing society members

  o Content: List of society members in each college's donor recognition list, or a symbol next to each member indicating society membership; should also include a brief explanation of what society is and how to become a member

  o Audience: Endowment, life-income, and estate gift donors (legacy donors)

  o Schedule: TBD

  o Budget: $0 (addition to existing publications at college level)

- Dean's/president's letter

  o Purpose: Thank society members for their ongoing support; inform members of addition of endowment donors to society

  o Content: Letter from the dean, updating society members for the college on goings-on, recent legacy gifts, impact of recent legacy gifts, and thanking for ongoing support

  o Audience: Society members affiliated with that specific college

  o Schedule: Complete by December 31

  o Budget: Estimated at $200

- Birthday card program

  o Purpose: Steward members

  o Content: Custom birthday card with photo showing impact of a legacy gift, with caption to explain why it is photographed; branded for society

  o Audience: Society members

  o Schedule: New version each fiscal year

  o Budget: $2,000

- National Philanthropy Day/Thanksgiving Day/ holiday card program

- o Purpose: Steward members

- o Content: Custom holiday or Thanksgiving Day card with photo showing impact of a legacy gift, with caption to explain why it is photographed; branded for society

- o Audience: Society members

- o Schedule: New version each fiscal year; mail on November 1

- o Budget: $800

- New Member Recognition Gift

  - o Purpose: Public recognition of members

  - o Content: Many options including: certificate of membership, pin, paperweight, mug, clock, picture frame, coasters, or something creative tied to GPD; note that most charities have a giveaway that does not tie to their mission—if you can create something mission driven or tied to the name of the society in a memorable and meaningful way, it will be appreciated. You want something your donors can hang on the wall, display, or wear

  - o Audience: New society members

  - o Schedule: October

  - o Budget: $2,000

- Existing Member recognition gift

  - o Purpose: Thank existing members for their ongoing support each year

  - o Content: Something useful that will spread the name of the society—some options include note cards, sticky notes, chocolates, wristbands, hats, pens, photo albums, etc.

  - o Audience: Existing society members

  - o Schedule: April

  - o Budget: $3,000

- Events

  - o Reunion weekend reception

    - Purpose: Steward society members

    - Content: Thank-you speech from director, including highlights of outcomes created by legacy gifts

    - Audience: Society members

    - Schedule: Annual—June 14

    - Budget: $5,000

o Other university events

- o Purpose: Steward and recognize Society members; Invite Society members to ALL University events for high-end donors, except annual fund recognition events (unless they have given at appropriate level for that year)

- o Content: No formal program; instead provide a small token of recognition, such as putting a special Society label/ribbon on the name tag; also may include free/valet parking; special reception area, etc.

- o Audience: Society members

- o Schedule: TBD

- o Budget: $200

- Society luncheon

  - o Purpose: Steward Society members

  - o Content: Thank-you speech from University President, including highlights of outcomes created by legacy gifts and success/impact of the program over time (luncheon should change locations each year to highlight legacy gifts at each of the Colleges over time); announce new members and deceased members

  - o Audience: Society members

  - o Schedule: Annual-April 19

  - o Budget: $12,500

Personalize. Personalize. Personalize!

On my most recent birthday, I received birthday cards from about half of the organizations I have included in my plans. Of those cards, only a few were hand-signed and included a personal note. The majority were preprinted without any personalization whatsoever. The one that caught my eye, however, was the one signed by an administrative assistant (who I helped to hire) in the name of the gift officer with whom I have a long-standing relationship. It certainly did not make me feel as though my gift was important to him or the organization. There is little point in sending out cards unless they are personalized. After all, several retailers sent me generic cards for the holidays last year, too.

—Brian

 stories from the real world

Gift Planning Marketing Grid

The sample marketing plan is likely more than you will need for your organization to start. Rather than use the entire plan, pick and choose those elements your organization can reasonably accomplish and place them on the gift planning marketing grid. The grid is a spreadsheet that has each of the traditional moves management steps. You can use the timeline to fill in a gift planning marketing plan on a month-by-month basis. If you have items that you plan to work on in years two or three, you can add them to the spreadsheet in a different color, or add an additional sheet for subsequent years. The idea is to create a simple document that can be used as a reference each month to create your to-do list for gift planning marketing.

Gift Planning Marketing Grid FY__												
	January	February	March	April	May	June	July	August	September	October	November	December
Identifying & Segmenting Prospects												
Educating Prospects												
Cultivating Prospects												
Soliciting Prospects												
Stewarding Donors												

Gift Planning Marketing Tracking Report

With your plan in place and marketing grid populated, the final step is tracking the performance of your gift planning effort on a month-by-month and year-by-year basis. Sometimes gift planning responses take years to materialize. Your organization should code each gift planning marketing piece so you can track which pieces and forms of outreach are most effective.

The template tracking report includes responses and known gifts from each marketing piece. Over time, you can add up these responses to show yearly results to determine which mechanisms are working for your organization and which ones should be replaced.

Gift Planning Marketing Tracking Report FY __												
	January	February	March	April	May	June	July	August	September	October	November	December
First Postcard												
Responses												
Known Gifts												
Winter Magazine Ad												
Responses												
Known Gifts												
January Gift Planning Tip of the Month												
Responses												
Known Gifts												

To Recap

◆ The best gift planning results come from one-on-one conversations with prospective gift planning donors. Use marketing to reach targeted and general audiences you cannot talk to personally.

◆ A gift planning marketing plan, utilizing a moves management platform, will drive your marketing efforts for loyal prospects and those interested in your mission in a focused way.

◆ Use the gift planning marketing grid to create an easy-to-follow, one-page document that serves as your to-do list for gift planning marketing, to ensure it is completed each month.

◆ Create a gift planning marketing tracking grid to evaluate the performance of your gift planning efforts over time.

Glossary

Actuarial—As used in planned giving, the factors used to calculate the value of lifetime payments to individuals or organizations.

Appreciated Property—Securities, real estate, or any other property that has risen in value since the benefactor acquired it. Generally, appreciated property held by an individual for more than a year may be donated at full fair market value with no capital gains cost.

Annuity—A contractual arrangement to pay a fixed sum of money to an individual at regular intervals. A charitable gift annuity is a gift to benefit an organization that secures fixed lifetime payments to the donor and/or another individual.

Adjusted Gross Income ("AGI")—The sum of an individual's taxable income for the year is the total at the bottom of the first page of IRS Form 1040. Your client may deduct outright charitable cash contributions up to 50 percent of AGI and outright gifts of appreciated securities and appreciated property or other gifts "for the use of" a charitable organization up to 30 percent of AGI. Any excess deduction may be carried over for up to five years following the year of the gift.

Attorney-in-Fact—An individual who is legally authorized to act on behalf of another by a power of attorney.

Appraisal—An assessment of the value of a piece of property. Benefactors contributing real or tangible personal property (art, books, collectibles, etc.) must secure an independent, qualified appraisal of the property to substantiate the value they claim as a charitable deduction.

Bargain Sale—When an individual sells property to a charity for less than its market value. Tax law considers this part sale and part charitable gift with tax benefits and capital gain apportioned to each part.

Basis—The benefactor's purchase price for an asset, possibly adjusted to reflect subsequent costs or depreciation. If your donor buys stock for $100 per share, the cost basis in the stock is $100 per share.

Beneficiary—The recipient of a bequest from a will or a distribution from a trust, life insurance policy, or retirement plan.

Bequest—A transfer of property or cash to an individual or organization under a will. A "bequest" may also refer more informally to an end-of-life distribution from a living trust, life insurance policy, or retirement plan.

Capital Gains Tax—A federal tax on the appreciation of a capital asset when it is sold.

Carryover—The portion of a charitable contribution that is not deductible for income tax purposes in the current year, but may be "carried over" and deducted in the following years for up to five years.

Codicil—A simple amendment to a will that avoids the cost and complication of rewriting the entire will. The codicil must be signed and witnessed or notarized according to the formalities required by the state of domicile.

Cost Basis—See Basis, above.

Cy-Pres—A court directive that saves an invalid charitable gift by giving it to another qualified charity that most nearly preserves the decedent's (donor's) charitable objective.

Decedent—A deceased person, especially one who has died lately.

Durable General Power of Attorney—A document by which an individual (known as the "principal") legally appoints another individual as her "attorney-in-fact" or "agent" for financial matters. The appointed person maintains the ability to oversee the principal's financial affairs even in the event of incapacity or disability.

Endowment Fund—The permanently held capital of a charity, the income (or a board approved spending policy of some percentage of the assets) from which is used to support ongoing projects and meet institutional needs.

Estate Tax—A federal tax on the value of the property transferred by an individual at his or her death (typically paid by individual's estate). Some states assess their own estate taxes as well.

Executor/trix or Personal Representative—The person named in a will or appointed by the probate court to administer the estate under the supervision of the probate court.

Fair Market Value—The price that an asset would bring in a sale from a willing seller to a willing buyer.

Grantor—The individual transferring property into a trust.

Health Care Power of Attorney—A document by which an individual known as the "principal" legally appoints another individual as her "Attorney-in-Fact" or "Agent" for health care decisions. The agent can make decisions about the principal's medical treatment in the event the principal is unable to do so.

Heir—The individual who is entitled to inherit property from a deceased individual in the absence of a will distributing the property otherwise. Every state has an intestacy statute defining who qualifies as heirs.

Income/Payment Interest—In a trust, the right to receive payments from the trust for life or a term of years.

Income in Respect of a Decedent (IRD)—Taxable income earned by a decedent that was not yet received before death. The most common IRD assets are IRAs and qualified retirement plans. Income tax will be assessed on those assets after the decedent's death and in the hands of beneficiaries.

Inter Vivos Gift—A gift made during the donor's lifetime.

Intestacy—When a person dies without a valid will, state laws will determine how the individual's probate estate will be divided by any heirs. If there are no heirs, then the state can claim any remaining probate assets.

IRA Charitable Rollover—The ability under the IRS code that allows a person to make a gift by transferring up to $100,000 annually from an IRA to a nonprofit organization without penalty or tax.

Joint Ownership—The ownership of property by two or more persons. If owned with "rights of survivorship," the property passes by operation of law to the surviving joint owner on a joint owner's death. In that case, the decedent's will does not control disposition of the property.

K-1 and 1099-R—The IRS forms sent to life-income gift income beneficiaries detailing how payments they received from their gifts during the year will be taxed.

Life-Income Gift—A planned gift that makes payments to the donor and/or other beneficiaries for life or a term of years, then distributes the remainder to charity.

Living Trust/Revocable Living Trust—A trust that is created by a living individual (grantor) that is used to manage assets for the benefit of the grantor and/or other persons. At the grantor's death the assets in the trust are passed to named beneficiaries, either outright or in further trust.

Living Will—A legal document that allows an individual to indicate whether or not she would like her life to be artificially prolonged in the event she is in a terminal or persistent vegetative state. A living will is often used in conjunction with a health care power of attorney, which appoints someone to make health care decisions on an individual's behalf.

Payable-on-Death (POD) Account—A special type of bank account that is recognized under state law which can be set up for checking, savings, and money market accounts, certificates of deposit and US savings bonds. A POD account allows the account owner to use a beneficiary designation form to name one or more designated beneficiaries to receive the assets in the account at the death of the account owner, with the assets passing outside of the probate process. The beneficiaries need only present the account manager with an original death certificate to claim the assets.

Personal Representative—See Executor, above.

Planned Giving/Gift Planning—The process of charitable giving in light of financial, estate and/or tax planning. Such gifts often require the assistance of an attorney, financial professional, or planned giving officer.

Pour-Over Will—A will used in conjunction with a living trust. The will directs that any property still owned by the decedent at the time of death "pours over" into the trust.

Probate Court—The court that determines the validity of a will and provides judicial oversight in the distribution of the estate. The "probate process" or "going through probate" refers to this court-supervised process. If there is no valid will, the probate court will appoint an administrator of the estate to facilitate the estate's distribution in accordance with state intestacy law.

Qualified Appraisal—A written appraisal prepared by a knowledgeable professional to determine the fair market value of property (other than marketable securities) donated to a charity. If the donor wishes to use the value of the donated property for a charitable income tax deduction, the appraisal must be obtained by the donor and attached to the tax return on which the deduction is claimed, if the property has a value of $5,000 or more. There are stringent educational requirements that a proposed "qualified appraiser" must meet, and the qualified appraisal must be prepared according to a detailed list of requirements set forth in the Internal Revenue Code and accompanying US Treasury regulations. When a qualified appraisal is required, the opinion of value of a curator, artist, real estate broker, or similar individual is not sufficient to support a claimed charitable deduction.

Remainder Interest—In a trust, the portion of the principal left after the payment interest has been paid to the noncharitable beneficiaries. A charitable remainder trust makes distributions to one or more individuals and then passes its remainder to charity. A gift of a remainder interest in real estate allows the entire property to pass to charity once the life estate holder has died.

Related-Use Rule—A donor can receive an income tax charitable deduction for the full fair market value of donated tangible personal property during life only if the property can be used by the charity in a way that is related to its tax-exempt purpose. Otherwise, the deduction is limited to the donor's cost basis. The related-use rule does not apply to transfers at death.

Remainder Beneficiary—A legal term for the individual or organization that receives the trust principal after the payment interest has been satisfied.

Required Minimum Distribution (RMD)—The amount that the IRS requires a person to withdraw each year from an IRA whether the funds are needed or not.

Residuum—The portion of a charitable gift annuity that remains for charity once the annuity payments terminate.

Right of Survivorship—A type of titling arrangement by which assets will automatically transfer from one person to another upon the death of the first person. See Joint Ownership.

Stepped-up Basis—When an individual inherits property from a decedent, the property's cost basis is stepped up to its fair market value on the date of death. The beneficiary receiving the property would avoid any capital gains tax if the property were to be immediately sold.

Tangible Personal Property—Artwork, collectibles, equipment, and other three-dimensional items. Tangible personal property does not include securities, business interests, or other interests represented on paper or electronically.

Testamentary Gift—A gift made by the donor from their estate after death.

Testamentary Trust—A trust that is created and goes into effect only when an individual dies. Such a trust is usually set up under the terms of a will.

Testator/Testatrix—The individual making a will.

Transfer-on-Death (TOD) Asset—A special type of investment asset that is recognized under state law which allows the owner to use a beneficiary designation form to name one or more designated beneficiaries to receive the assets at the death of the owner, with the assets passing outside of the probate process. The beneficiaries need only present an original death certificate to claim the assets. Some states also recognize TOD deeds for the transfer of real estate.

Trust—A separate legal entity created when a grantor transfers property to the care of an individual **or organizational trustee for the benefit of one or more beneficiaries.**

Trustee—An individual or organization exercising fiduciary power to carry out the wishes of the person who established a trust (the "grantor") as stated in the trust document.

Will Contest—The formal process for challenging the validity of a will.

Index

This is the *Getting Started in Charitable Gift Planning: The Resource Book.* Be sure to pick up *Getting Started in Charitable Gift Planning: Your Guide to Planned Giving,* published by CharityChannel Press as part of the popular **In the Trenches**™ series for nonprofit-sector practitioners.

Getting Started in Charitable Gift Planning

Your Guide to Planned Giving

Brian M. Sagrestano, JD, CFRE

Robert E. Wahlers, MS, CFRE

Your guide to planned giving that will:

- Help you to understand gift planning in the 21st century
- Outline the best infrastructure for a donor-focused gift planning program
- Assist you in identifying and developing prospects for planned gifts
- Guide you in creating a marketing plan to effectively grow your donor relationships
- Provide helpful tips from the field

CharityChannel.com/bookstore

Charity Channel
PRESS™

You also might be interested in our just-released *CharityChannel's Quick Guide to Developing Your Case for Support,* by Margaret Guellich and Linda Lysakowski.

*Charity*Channel's®
Quick Guide to™

Developing Your Case for Support

Margaret Guellich, CFRE
Linda Lysakowski, ACFRE

- Learn what a case for support is, and isn't
- Determine who should write your case for support
- Prepare to gather all the information you need to write your case
- Build a case that tells your story to your various "publics"

CharityChannel.com/bookstore

*Charity*Channel®
PRESS™

Did you know that CharityChannel Press is the fastest growing publisher of books for busy nonprofit professionals? Here are some of our most popular titles.

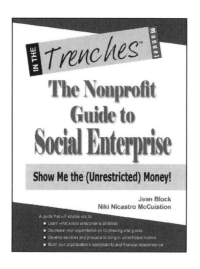

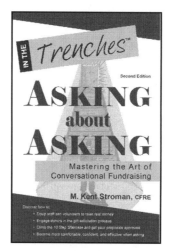

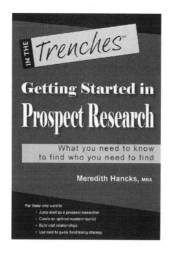

CharityChannel.com/bookstore

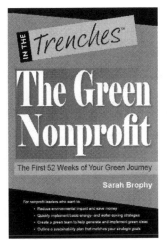

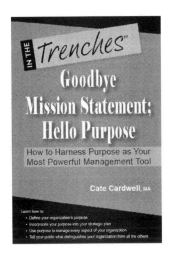
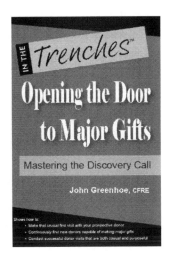

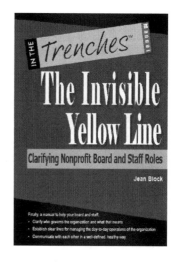

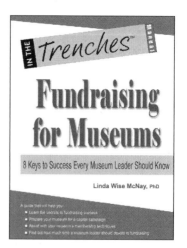

CharityChannel.com/bookstore

And now introducing **For the GENIUS® Press,** an imprint that produces books on just about any topic that people want to learn. You don't have to be a genius to read a **GENIUS** book, but you'll sure be smarter once you do!

ForTheGENIUS.com/bookstore

Grantsmanship

for the GENIUS

A master grantwriter and
a veteran funder reveal
the keys to winning grants

Goodwin Deacon
Ken Ristine

FOR THE GENIUS IN ALL OF US

ForTheGENIUS.com/bookstore

PRESS

Nonprofit Board Service

for the GENIUS®

Find the right board, sharpen your skills, and become a stellar board member

Susan Schaefer, CFRE

Bob Wittig, MBA

FOR THE GENIUS IN ALL OF US™

ForTheGENIUS.com/bookstore

for the GENIUS
PRESS

Made in the USA
Lexington, KY
06 December 2018